D0790881

FELLOWSHIP BIBLE CHURCH
16391 CHILLICOTHE ROAD
CHAGRIN FALLS, OH 44023-4323

HiS
GUIDE TO
EVANGELISM

PAUL E. LITTLE & OTHERS

InterVarsity Press
Downers Grove
Illinois 60515

Second printing, January 1978

© 1977 by Inter-Varsity Christian Fellowship
of the United States of America.
All rights reserved. No part of this book
may be reproduced in any form without
written permission from InterVarsity Press.

Articles printed here originally appeared in
HIS magazine, published monthly October through
June, © 1972, 1973, 1974, 1975, 1976 by
Inter-Varsity Christian Fellowship
of the United States of America. To subscribe
write HIS magazine, 5206 Main Street,
Downers Grove, Illinois 60515.

InterVarsity Press is the book publishing division
of Inter-Varsity Christian Fellowship, a
student movement active on campus at hundreds of
universities, colleges and schools of nursing.
For information about local and regional
activities, write IVCF, 233 Langdon St.,
Madison, WI 53703.

ISBN 0-87784-488-7
Library of Congress Catalog
Card Number: 77-72523

Printed in the United States of America

CONTENTS

PART 1 THE CONTEXT

1/Before You Pass It On   11
Paul E. Little

2/What Is Evangelism?   15
John W. Alexander

PART 2 THE MESSAGE

3/Know the News   21
Allen Harris

4/Say Why You Believe   31
Kenneth Harper

PART 3 TALKING ABOUT JESUS

5/Meet Them Where They Are   39
Bill Tiffan

6/Strategic Conversations   43
Mark Pettersen

7/Sharing Christ, Ourselves   49
and Pizza...All at Once
Becky Manley

8/Campus Casualty: A Case   70
Study
C. Stephen Board

9/Encouraging a Decision   74
Paul E. Little

PART 4 EVANGELISTIC LIFESTYLE

10/How to Develop an Evangelistic Lifestyle   83
Terrell Smith

11/Friendship Evangelism   94
Paul Tokunaga

12/Home: How to Be Salt to Your Family without Rubbing It In   97
Janet Carter

13/Jesus Made Disciples   107
Mike Hayes

14/The Last Step Is the First   114
William York

PART 5 CAMPUS STRATEGY

15/Spying Out the Land   125
Andrew T. LePeau

16/Translating the Gospel into Greek   131
Edward Focht

17/Group Witness   139
Don Smith

18/A Case Study in Campus Evangelism: Miami U. of Ohio   143
C. Stephen Board

Tools for Evangelism   152

Christianity, as someone has said, has never been a spectator sport. Every Christian believer is a part of the body of Christ which represents God to the world. And every believer is—like it or not—a witness of one sort or other concerning what God is like.

While we sometimes shy away from it, having a pass-along faith is actually a great thing. What better favor could you do for a friend or neighbor than to communicate (in show-and-tell fashion) the greatness of God's love? Most of us are believers today primarily because someone else personally showed and told *us*.

This book is the collected wisdom of sixteen people who have had experience (most of them in association with Inter-Varsity Christian Fellowship) in sharing the gospel and training others to do so. Each of the articles first appeared in HIS magazine, aimed at helping college and university students. The principles are easily adaptable to a church program or to any situation in which you are studying and practicing evangelism.

Linda Doll, Editor, HIS magazine

PART 1
THE CONTEXT

BEFORE YOU PASS IT ON
PAUL E. LITTLE

1

Many people either do not get started in witnessing or do not get anywhere because they have the wrong attitudes.

Scripture says that our attitude is crucial in everything we do: "Be transformed by the renewal of your mind" (Rom. 12:2). Our thoughts and attitudes determine our actions.

What attitudes should we have about witnessing?

genuine enthusiasm First, we must be convinced that being a Christian is the greatest thing in the world. Once we are persuaded of that, we will know that the greatest favor we can do anyone is to introduce him to Jesus Christ. We need genuine en thusiasm about our personal relationship with Jesus Christ. If we do not have this attitude, witnessing will be a constant drag, something we have to do, not something we want to do.

How do we get this attitude? It begins with total commitment to Jesus Christ. A half-committed Christian (if there is such a thing) cannot help being unhappy. He is not sold out to anything. But the Christian who can honestly say with Paul, "To me to live is Christ," can have the same joy Paul had. It also comes with appreciating what Christ has given us. Too many of us, particularly if we have been raised in a Christian environment, have taken for granted what we have as Christians. Sometimes we feel cheated. We think non-Christians are having a ball and secretly envy them.

We Christians need to ask ourselves, "Where would I be if Christ had never entered my life?" Think about it and you may find yourself surprisingly thankful. Ask yourself, "What does Christ mean to me today?" Do not ask what he is supposed to mean, but what he actually does mean. Does he give any sense of purpose? Is there any peace from knowing him? Do you sense any power in your life which is not your own? You may be surprised to realize all the things for which you have not been thankful recently.

Think of some non-Christians you know who have none of these and are giving their whole lives to things that end with the grave. If you do not know anyone like this, make a deliberate attempt to get to know some non-Christians on your campus. Many students are very open about their despair and aimlessness in life. Popular music and the drama frequently state this in eloquent terms. You cannot help but be enthusiastic when you know you have the answer. Your enthusiasm will be even greater when you see someone become a Christian and pass from death to life.

motivation A second important attitude will grow out of the first. We witness out of love for Christ and others, not to accumulate spiritual brownie points and advance our own status as Christians. Loving non-Christians means that we desire their best. We do not swoon over them sentimentally. We show we love Christ when we obey him (Jn. 14:21), and one of his clearest commands is that we share the faith (Mt. 28:19-20).

If we are convinced that we are doing other people a favor by witnessing to them, we will not be threatened if they do not respond. We will be saved from the begging which often demeans the gospel. They will realize we are not using them to advance ourselves, which they would resent, but genuinely want to share the best thing we have found in life. They are the losers if they turn it down.

A third attitude is realizing that God is the evangelist and we are his instruments. Even though we are God's only mouth and feet, the whole thing does not depend on us. The Holy Spirit creates spiritual interest. We cannot create it, we can only discover it. God the Holy Spirit converts people. All we can do is issue the invitation. This realization will deliver us from fear on the one hand. No one is beyond God's power. If a person understands and then rejects the gospel, he is refusing God—not us. This also saves us from pride. We may have the privilege of being the last link in the chain bringing a person to Christ, yet it is no credit to us because God gave the increase (1 Cor. 3:6). We do not measure our spirituality by how many scalps we have. At the same time, we are alert to issue the invitation at every possible opportunity.

imperfect messengers If God is the evangelist and we are his instruments, perfection is not required to witness. God even used Balaam's ass to convey a message when he had to. If we desire to please the Lord and try to live a consistent life, we must not allow the enemy to seal our lips by overwhelming us with an awareness of our failures. We do not invite people to become Christians because we are perfect, but because Jesus Christ is perfect. If we make ourselves hypocrites, no one will listen. If we show that we are sinners saved by grace, other sinners will be attracted.

Finally, we must believe that people are interested and will respond to quiet confidence. Most of us assume people are not interested and almost apologize for bringing up the subject. If we do not apologize, we are generally so nervous that the other person becomes nervous too.

We must learn to relax. Try explaining the gospel to a friend as a beginning. You might even practice talking as you would to a non-Christian. Stand in front of a mirror and watch yourself. Getting used to hearing your own voice can help you relax. Then take the plunge. Nothing will persuade you that people are interested until you are led by the Spirit to someone who is.

Paul E. Little, author of How to Give Away Your Faith, *served on Inter-Varsity staff from 1950 until his death in 1975. He was also Associate Professor of Evangelism at Trinity Evangelical Divinity School.*

WHAT IS EVANGELISM?

JOHN W. ALEXANDER

2

FELLOWSHIP BIBLE CHURCH
16391 CHILLICOTHE ROAD
CHAGRIN FALLS, OH 44023-4323

One of the most common words among Christians is the word "evangelism." What is the biblical meaning of this word?

The words "evangelism" and "evangelize" do not appear in English New Testaments. However, "evangelist(s)" occurs three times: Acts 21:8 refers to a man who was an evangelist; 2 Timothy 4:5 is a charge to do the work of an evangelist; and Ephesians 4:11 says that God endows some people with the special gift of evangelizing.

To further clarify matters, two significant words occur frequently in Greek New Testaments. *Euangelion*, the first word, is a noun meaning "good news" or "gospel." God has carried out his plan of exalting his Son to save sinners. *Euangelizomai,* the second word, is a verb meaning "to announce good news," "to proclaim the gospel."

Based on this information, we can define evangelism as the attempt to perform two services:

1/*Making the gospel message known.* Here we aim at people's minds so that they may be informed about God and their relationship to him, what God has done to improve that relationship and what they must do to respond properly to God's action.

For this communication to be successful, our statements must be clear (Col. 4:4) and sufficiently understood. But here we face the severe problem of outside interference which is described in 2 Corinthians 4:3-4. Therefore, our prayer must be that we receive adequate power from the Lord himself (Col. 4:2-4).

2/*Seeking to convert.* Here we aim at people's wills so that they will act on the above information. We persuade people to act.

Thus, if we are able to evangelize we need both a burning heart and a clear mind. Biblical evangelism includes both of these principles. Declaration without persuasion can be sterile and dead. Persuasion without proper declaration can be dangerous.

Declaration without persuasion is simply instruction. It can be factually correct and informationally complete, but if all it does is communicate information—be it ever so clear—it is no more than instruction. A person who does only this may be a good instructor, but he or she is certainly not an evangelist.

Nor is persuasion itself enough. I can urge, cajole and do everything in my power to persuade someone to become a Christian. But no matter how earnest my endeavors, persuasion is still merely exhortation. A person who only exhorts, no matter how eloquently, may be a mover of people, but he is not an evangelist.

If I am to do the work of an evangelist, I should be active both in communicating clearly the gospel of Jesus Christ and in persuading men to respond to that message. This is the biblical standard of evangelism.

John W. Alexander, author of Managing Our Work *and* Practical Criticism, *is the President of Inter-Varsity Christian Fellowship of the United States of America.*

PART 2
THE MESSAGE

KNOW THE NEWS
ALLEN HARRIS

3

If you think you can skip this article because you know the Christian message, then this is for you. If you are anxious to read it because your main hang-up in evangelism is that you do not know what to say to people when the big opportunity comes, then maybe this will help.

We live in a day of methods. By and large our evangelism has become method-centered. Christians have memorized a few clichés and think they have the message under their Bible belt. All we need, we are told, are better methods or more creative ideas to present the gospel. So we have conference after conference on methods of evangelism, while the church becomes weaker and weaker in its understanding of the message and ability to communicate it.

We have forgotten that the New Testament defines "to evangelize" as "to tell/declare/announce good news." News. That means content. God wants us to major on the *message*. If we do not, our evangelism is like an elaborately designed book with blank pages. We must know what the gospel is before we can be effective evangelists.

tools and scripts To that end, I will suggest an outline of the gospel. But it is not to be memorized and plugged into people as a standard script-method for two reasons.

First, did you ever notice that no chapter in the Bible contains a neat outline of all the elements of the gospel? Did you ever wonder why? After all, it would make evangelism so much easier. But that is just the point. We would all plug that chapter in as a super method. And God wants us to see that the gospel is the whole Bible, Genesis to Revelation. Our gospel should be a summary of God's entire message to a lost world. My outline is designed to help you expand your understanding of God's message, so that as you saturate yourself in his Word (Old Testament too!), you will communicate from your growing understanding of his infinitely rich message.

I always suggest that people make this outline their own by using a topical Bible and concordance, expanding each point with additional verses that they find helpful. I visited one student's room a month after suggesting this to him. On his table I discovered the outline and nine or ten pages of Scripture verses for the four points, which he had begun to memorize. God used that student mightily in an evangelistic outreach.

Two students from the U. of Maryland created a multimedia presentation of the gospel with nearly one hundred texts of Scripture under the points and subpoints. One of them said, "Now I feel the message is mine." There is power in his evangelism.

Second, we cannot use this or any other presentation as a standard script because people are not standard. One is a pure relativist, another very complacent and a third near despair under a weight of guilt. We are called to meet people where they are. Have you ever noticed that Jesus never dealt with any two people the same way? In John 3 he hits Nicodemus between the eyes ("You must be born again"), but the next chapter finds him using a very different, less direct tactic with the woman at the well. God calls you and me to be spiritual doctors, to listen to people, discerning where they are spiritually, so we can approach them with the gospel and emphasize the elements necessary for them to have a clear picture of their root problem and God's radical solution.

This outline, then, is a tool for you to use to organize and amplify your thoughts and make sure you have presented the whole message faithfully. When you understand the gospel, you will both listen and communicate more effectively.

The gospel is a message with four main points: God, man, Christ and response. Modern men and women must understand something about each of these areas in order to make a true commitment to Christ.

god as the holy creator We cannot start with

Christ since he makes no sense apart from the problem of sin which he came to deal with. But we cannot start with sin, for sin makes no sense apart from the Creator God whose nature we have violated and whose majesty we have assaulted. And we cannot assume that people in the twentieth century have a biblical notion of God just because they use the word *God.* So we must tell them enough about God to make them realize that God has an absolute claim on their lives.

We speak of an infinite God who brought all things into being out of nothing, creating and sustaining us of his own free will so that we are utterly dependent on him for everything (Gen. 1—2; Acts 17:25, 28; Is. 40:28; Ps. 100:3). Thus God's basic nature is not love, but (if anything in him could ever be called basic) Creator. From this base comes two mighty pillars of his being, as seen in the diagram.

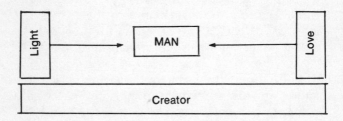

These pillars are light and love. Light is one of the richest images in the Bible and speaks of God's majesty, truth, holiness and purity (1 Jn. 1:5; 1 Tim. 6:15-16; Is. 40:12-13; 42:8; 45:5, 18-23; Ps. 135, 136, 139). God's transcendent holiness is apparent. But this God is also personal. Out of his love he created us in his image so that we could commune with him and worship him. Worship is the only appropriate response of the creature to the Creator (Gen. 1:26-27; 2:7; Deut. 6:4-5; Lk. 10:27).

In the beginning God's light and love both rested upon us and we were free to fulfill all our potential as the creatures in God's image. This is what God intended.

sinful creatures We blew it and willfully rebelled. This is called sin. We must both define sin and state its consequences. Sin is essentially two things. First, sin is playing God—not acknowledging God as our God. I am my own god (Gen. 3:5) and live as if God did not matter. Romans 1:21 describes sin as not worshiping God, not even being thankful, and creating my own handy, pocket-sized god who lets me center on myself. We deny what God has told us about himself.

Second, sin is fighting God—breaking his law, a reflection of his nature and our standard of behavior as his creatures. We need to use the ten commandments more in our evangelism. We need to help people know the guilt of sin before they will desire the forgiveness found in Christ. Helpful verses: 1 John 3:4; Romans 3:12; 8:6-8; Isaiah 53:6; 64:6; James 2:10; 1 Samuel 16:7; Jeremiah 17:9.

The consequence of sin is death. In the Bible this means separating the two elements which, when joined together, are life. Physical death is separation from the body. Symptoms are disease and physical suffering. Spiritual death is separation from God for eternity. Symptoms now are selfishness, hatred, wars, alienation, loneliness. Helpful verses: Isaiah 59:2; Ezekiel 18:4, 20; Romans 6:23; Ephesians 2:1-3.

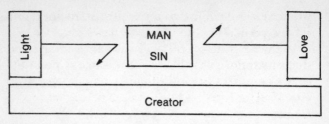

How can God be light, and still love people who have rebelled against him and broken his law? This would violate God's justice. In fact, if one person ever sinned and got away with it, God would no longer be God, for he would not be just.

This new relationship is illustrated above. Love and light are now in tension and conflict.

christ the merciful redeemer If you read the Old Testament you see clearly that Jesus Christ came to fulfill the three roles of prophet, priest and king. In fact, these roles were pictures of Christ's work as our redeemer. American evangelism in the last hundred years has tended to speak only of his office of priest or Savior. This has led to superficial evangelism and decisions for Christ as an insurance policy.

We must present Jesus in all three roles. In a rough way these focus respectively on his perfect life, sacrificial death and victorious resurrection. We must tell people of God-become-man who lived for thirty-three years on earth, the only one who ever loved the Lord his God with all his heart, and his neighbor as himself. As prophet, he revealed God by his teachings and life (Deut. 18:15-19; Jn. 1:14-18; 7:16-24; 8:28; 12:49-50; 14:24).

Therefore, he alone could be my priest to offer himself as a substitutionary sacrifice, take my guilt upon him and die for my sins. The priest represented the people to God. Jesus represented me.

We must present the cross not simply as a vague demonstration of God's love, but as the place in history where, in the death of his Son, God judged the sins of all those who are united in a relationship with Christ.

God is still just and holy (light), for he can love me in Christ who took my sin and gave me his righteousness.

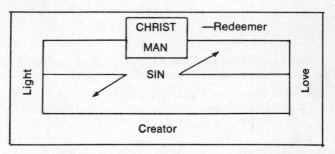

Verses dealing with his sacrifice: Isaiah 53:4-7; Matthew 26:28; John 2:19-21; Galatians 2:20; 1 Peter 2:24; 3:18; Hebrews 7:27; 9:11-14, 22-26; 10:10; 1 John 4:10.

Finally, we must tell of his resurrection as King. He has conquered death. The New Testament refers to Jesus as *Savior* 24 times, but calls him *Lord* 694 times—more than 28 times for every reference as *Savior*. We must be clear that all who will have Jesus as priest must also have him as their King. This was the purpose of his resurrection and ascension. Jesus now lives to rule his people in love so that they become more like him as members of his eternal kingdom. Helpful verses: Matthew 26:64; Acts 2:32-36; Philippians 2:9-11; 1 Corin- **27** thians 15:20-28; Revelation 5:11-14.

the necessary response All we have said so far is history. The question now is: If my only hope is to be united to Christ in his finished work as prophet, priest and King, how do I become united to Christ? The answer is to repent and believe in Christ. Since these are loaded words, I find it better to speak of turning to and trusting in Christ.

We must urge people to turn with their minds, emotions and wills by acknowledging that they are guilty rebels with no defense, deserving God's judgment. They must hate their rebellion and determine to forsake it to serve God as Lord of their lives. Here we must be careful to differentiate between people who simply feel like zeros because of inferiority complexes, and the ones who see that they are infinitely significant even as rebels, but know guilt before God because of their rebellion. Only the latter ones are truly turning to Christ.

As people realize that they can never do anything to make themselves acceptable before God, we invite them to *trust* in Christ and rest in him as Savior and Lord with their whole selves. Invite and urge them to commit their lives to Christ and cast themselves upon him. Scriptures that are useful here include John 1:12; 3:16; Ephesians 2:8-9; Galatians 2:16, 20; Acts 16:30-31. I have found 1 John 5:11-13 especially helpful at this point.

Finally, we need to make clear that people cannot even turn from sin and trust in God by themselves, but the Holy Spirit must enable them. This never comes as a surprise to a person under true conviction of sin.

Four final things to remember in sharing the message:

1/*Use your Bible.* Have the person you are talking to read the text to himself and explain to you what he thinks about its meaning. Many times this has been the turning point in my sharing the message with people. It prevents tangents and arguments, confronting the person with God's authority, not yours. James 1:18 and 1 Peter 1:23 say we are born again by the written Word of God, so let us put people in direct contact with it.

2/*Memorize Scripture* and Scripture references so you can give the appropriate portion of God's Word for that person. Use Dr. Alexander's *Scripture Memory 101* or some other aid.

3/*Pray.* Our message seems foolish to the non-Christian and if we really believe that only the Holy Spirit can make them respond, we will pray—before, during and after our talk.

4/*Communicate* absolute biblical concepts clearly so that the person does not read his or her own ideas into them (for example, Christ as superpsychiatrist). Be careful that the individual knows you are speaking about absolute truth, not just your opinion or "truth-for-me." Francis Schaeffer's books are helpful here.

Paul says in 2 Corinthians 2:14-17 that people are never the same again for eternity after we have shared this powerful message with them. Who then is qualified for such a responsibility? He answers boldly that we are, "For we are not, like so many, peddlers of an adulterated message of God, but from the purest motives before God we speak in Christ as those sent from God" (Berkeley). Be warned: Is your message faithful to the Word of

God in content and emphasis? Be encouraged: God did not commission tape recorders to evangelize so he could have "the perfect message." You will make mistakes as I do. But if your motives are pure and you seek to be faithful to God's message, God will teach as you go and give you fruit to his glory.

Allen Harris is an Inter-Varsity staff member in Syracuse, New York. He graduated from Westminster Theological Seminary.

SAY WHY YOU BELIEVE
KENNETH HARPER

4

Recently a friend of mine was invited to participate in a conference for Christians. He worked hard on the two papers he was asked to present, setting forth an intelligent defense of Christianity. When he arrived at the conference, the others suggested that intellectual issues be set aside and turned the whole gathering into a Christian sensitivity session. In such an atmosphere it was almost impossible to deal with relevant issues.

Apologetics, the art of intellectually defending Christianity, is largely ignored in our day. Today most Christians emphasize the personal, emotional, gut-level Christianity that excludes intellectual matters. Unfortunately, this complete reliance on emotion is a shaky foundation for faith. In *The World's Last Night*, C. S. Lewis wrote that feelings cannot be our sole spiritual diet because it is physically and psychologically impossible to maintain a fixed emotional state. This is behind Jesus' command for a complete, balanced faith: "You shall love the Lord your God with all your heart [emotion], and with all your soul [commitment], and with all your mind [intellect]" (Mt. 22:37).

In today's world unbelievers may well call upon Christians to fulfill Peter's charge to "be prepared to make a defense to any one who calls you to account for the hope that is in you" (1 Pet. 3:15). A strong case for apologetics can be made from this one verse. The word used for "defense" (*apologia* in Greek) is a legal term which means the presentation of evidence to support your position.

apologetics in three parts Every Christian has a duty to represent Christ as well as he or she possibly can. Apologetics, which provides the tools for this task, has three categories.

First, we need to define precisely what the Christian gospel *is*. Often the unbeliever rejects a caricature or perversion of Christianity, not true Christianity. Knowing the content of faith can clear away the deadwood and allow important issues to surface. We need a mental list of priorities so that we do not wage intellectual warfare over secondary issues while letting more vital matters slip by unnoticed. Jesus' interaction with the Samaritan woman (Jn. 4) should be our model here. He guided her question about where she should worship, back to the more important issue of his own Messiahship.

Second, we must engage in the negative task of

showing the weaknesses, difficulties and contradictions in the non-Christian positions we encounter. This broad category includes at least three subdivisions. (1) Philosophical apologetics demonstrates the weaknesses of prevailing non-Christian philosophies (such as logical positivism, Marxism, existentialism, etc.). (2) Religious apologetics deals with the shortcomings of alternative religions (Hinduism, Zen Buddhism or modern cults). And (3) cultural apologetics seeks to show that the concepts underlying secular, twentieth-century culture, when extended to their logical conclusions, add up to zero.

The falsity of a non-Christian system does not automatically make the Christian position true. The apologist's third role is to provide positive evidence for the truth of Christianity. In the past, this evidence has come primarily from prophecy and miracles. Although prophecy has fallen into disuse, I am struck by the continuing truth of Pascal's statement, "Under the Christian religion, I find actual prophecy, and I find it in no other." Throughout the Old Testament, a prophet was evaluated by whether or not his prophecies came true. If they did, he was God's mouthpiece. If they did not, he was to be rejected (see Deut. 13 and 18). In the New Testament too, the effort is made, especially in Matthew's Gospel, to validate Jesus' authority by showing that Old Testament prophecies were fulfilled in him. That argument is still valid today.

The Christian's strongest evidence is the miraculous. Jesus and the apostles emphasized this. Jesus said that all his claims to deity and Messiahship hung on the miracle of the resurrection (Mt. 12: 39-40). And the apostles also saw this event as central to their message (1 Cor. 15:3-8). By marshalling the historical evidence on behalf of Christ's life, specifically the resurrection, the Christian can build a powerful case for the truth of the gospel.

To those two positive proofs, I would add what Francis Schaeffer calls the "final apologetic"—the changed lifestyle of the Christian. A missionary I know used to say, "Your lives are the only gospel some people will ever read: What do they see?" The apologetic of changed lives is both the easiest and the hardest to present—easiest because it requires no mastering of intellectual material, and hardest because it requires a daily surrender of life to God.

By sheer volume, the variety of apologetic methods outlined above may discourage potential apologists. Most people have far more pressing demands on their time than reading scores of books on apologetics. I can sympathize with this problem. When intellectual difficulties with my faith bothered me, reading apologetic works was so time-consuming that it contributed to a dismal grade-point average.

I propose a mini-library of ten paperbacks for apologetics. If they are read and kept handy for reference, they will supply a wealth of information on most apologetic issues that you are likely to encounter. The entire collection can be purchased for under $25.00, and should find a place on every educated Christian's bookshelf.

apologetic mini-library

(1) Gordon Lewis, *Decide for Yourself* (InterVarsity Press, $2.50). The author uses inductive studies from relevant Scripture passages to help the reader build a fully biblical theology.

(2) Colin Brown, *Philosophy and the Christian Faith* (InterVarsity Press, $5.95). Brown's work is histori-

cal as well as apologetic. Though brief, it contains many footnotes and a full bibliography to guide further research in specific areas.

(3) J. N. D. Anderson, *Christianity and Comparative Religion* (InterVarsity Press, $1.95). By showing the uniqueness in Christian concepts of God, revelation, salvation and ethics, Anderson provides a strong answer for those who claim that all religions are "saying the same thing in different ways."

(4) and (5) Francis Schaeffer, *Escape from Reason* and *The God Who Is There* (InterVarsity Press, $1.95 and $3.50). Francis Schaeffer is the best-known cultural apologist writing today. His nearly prophetic works show the bankruptcy of contemporary values and how Christianity can fill the resulting spiritual vacuum.

(6) Paul Little, *Know Why You Believe* (InterVarsity Press, $1.75). Little draws upon his wide experience in evangelism at colleges and universities to give chapter-length treatments of the most commonly met objections to Christianity.

(7) John Urquhart, *The Wonders of Prophecy* (Christian Publishers, $2.00). This work is a classic in its area. Though fifty years old, it remains the most complete treatment in print of fulfilled prophecy.

(8) John W. Montgomery, *History and Christianity* (InterVarsity Press, $1.95). Montgomery collects a wealth of historical evidence on behalf of Jesus' resurrection and explores its relevance to apologetics and theology.

(9) F. F. Bruce, *The New Testament Documents: Are They Reliable?* (InterVarsity Press, $1.50). Dr. Bruce is one of the finest New Testament scholars alive today. In this work he surveys the evidence of **35**

archaeology, secular first-century historians and manuscript transmission to conclude that the New Testament documents, as we have them, are the most reliable historical records of classical antiquity.

(10) C. S. Lewis, *Miracles: A Preliminary Study* (Macmillan, $1.45). One of the most bothersome elements of Christianity for those in the twentieth century is its inseparable connection with miracles. In his most philosophical work, C. S. Lewis presents a convincing case for accepting New Testament miracles.

Kenneth Harper is a graduate of Trinity Evangelical Divinity School and is currently an associate pastor at a church in Mount Holly, New Jersey.

PART 3
TALKING ABOUT JESUS

MEET THEM WHERE THEY ARE
BILL TIFFAN

5

Jim and Joe are strangers who meet in a restaurant. Jim is a Christian. After the usual light conversation involved in getting acquainted, Jim "feels led" to witness to Joe and ask him what he thinks of Jesus Christ. Depending on Joe's response, the conversation either suddenly grinds to a halt or continues. I consider this approach in evangelism "out of context."

By "context" I mean the sum of an individual's experience, such as education, church, friendships, jobs and family life, plus his or her values and beliefs. Refusing to take the time to discover elements of the context of someone's life is refusing to discover the person himself.

A second example. Carol and Sue are also strangers who meet one day, Carol being the Christian. Instead of raising the question of Jesus soon after they meet, Carol asks questions about Sue's background. Soon the two girls are in a lengthy two-way conversation. Based on what she learns about Sue's background, Carol comes to some conclusions about areas of need that Sue is probably experiencing. A few thoughtful questions from Carol put those conclusions to the test. She can then begin applying what she knows about Jesus Christ to Sue's situation. If her conclusions prove to be wrong, she just keeps asking more questions as time and the nature of the conversation allow.

Since both girls have been sharing about themselves, Sue interprets Carol's comments about Christ as being part of Carol herself (part of her context). She has a way to relate this information about Christianity to a real person. Sue has a basis for evaluating what she learns about Christ because she has a context in which to examine it.

This second example embodies several principles about relating to people. The most obvious is that Carol tried to learn the context of Sue's life. As their conversation continued, Carol and Sue found some common interests which formed bonds or bridges of communication in their relationship. Once these bridges were formed, Carol could then begin to interpret Sue's context and apply spiritual truths which were relevant. For example, suppose Carol discovered that no one at home ever affirmed Sue's worth as a person or showed her love. Carol could then interpret that fact by asking herself, "How would that affect her relationships with people outside her family? She probably would be skeptical of their love." Then Carol could apply spiritual truth by mentioning something about God's unconditional love that she herself has experienced. Maybe she would decide to spend time with Sue to demonstrate that she is worth something. In the first case Joe would learn about Christianity as a bare message without *seeing* how it works in a person's life. In the second case Sue could not only learn about the message, but could also see how it worked in Carol's life. If the two girls' contexts were fairly similar, Sue might say to herself, "It works for her—her life is similar to mine—maybe I should consider it." If Sue did accept Christ, the bonds between them would make her subsequent follow-up occur quite naturally.

Suppose instead of a brief meeting with a stranger you have a long-term opportunity for relating to a non-Christian, for example, as a roommate. What then? Basically the same approach is used except that you now have a longer time to understand your friend's context. You have more time to build bridges of communication to fuse your relationship. Strong bonds that consist of common interests are needed so that in the event your non-Christian friend rejects discussion about Jesus Christ, the relationship will still continue.

You need to be willing to continue relationships even when non-Christians say No to Christ. If they reject Christ and you reject them, they are left with the conclusion that the relationship was conditional. How can we have the attitude that our duty to love people is conditioned by their belief in Christ when Christ himself died, showing his love for us, while *we* were sinners and enemies of God (Rom. 5:8, 10)? Neglecting relationships with non-Chris- **41** tians is probably the best example of our failure to love as Christ loved us.

Bill Tiffan has been on staff with Inter-Varsity in San Diego for several years.

STRATEGIC CONVERSATIONS
MARK PETTERSEN

6

Convinced that personal evangelism should be an important part of your life? Great. But now that you are gung-ho, maybe you have run across a few snags like . . .

Your non-Christian friends will not be quiet long enough for you to tell them the gospel.

You get caught in circular conversations even though you have memorized "What Non-Christians Ask" (in chapter five of Paul Little's *How to Give Away Your Faith*).

Your non-Christian friends listen politely, but display little interest in your gospel diagrams.

Evangelism just is not for you.

All of the above

If you are experiencing any of these situations, your problem is not "what" but "how."

prefab talks just don't make it Christians have benefited greatly from the popular gospel summaries and outlines. They have helped us put our finger on the salient features of the gospel. Often, though, a lecture is not appropriate to the opportunities God gives us.

Another problem with simply blapping out a gospel package is that the presuppositions of the package sometimes do not fit the customer. How can you tell an atheist "God loves you," and still communicate that you understand his position? An agnostic friend of mine was approached by a Christian with the lecture approach. After the Christian made his first point, my friend objected that he was not ready to grant any God, let alone a God who loved him. But the Christian insisted they finish the outline before they discussed that issue. My friend was forced to listen to a presentation that obviously did not relate to him. The immediate effect was that he lost both warmth for the Christian as a person and freedom to ask further questions.

Some sensitive people may get the idea that you are a spiritual encyclopedia salesman because your talk has the same rehearsed sound.

These are just a few of the problems with a lecture approach to evangelism, but perhaps the best reason to move away from it is that there is a better way.

try ordinary conversation Conversation is one of the best ways to communicate any truth because it gets both parties involved in the action. It also allows ideas to be stated in a natural and personal manner, dealing with objections as they come up. But most of us fear this form of communication because we have no control over what will be discussed. We may be faced with questions and concepts we have not previously considered.

In any conversation, the content is controlled to a large extent by the questions. If you want to control what is discussed, then you must take the initiative in asking questions. But you say, What do I ask? To answer that, we should look at some possible topics of conversation.

The first topic that most people discuss is relationships. This deals with the question, Who are you? We answer this by revealing our relationship to a common known—a person, an institution, an activity or a location (for example, I'm Marsha's sister, I'm a freshman at the U. of Texas, I'm from Chicago).

If we remain in this first area only, it is a light conversation. If we are truly interested in the other person, we will usually move to a second area. This area I call dogma. It answers the question, What do you believe? Some people think only dogmatic people have dogmas or strong convictions. But everyone has a long list of beliefs about right and wrong, politics, God, love and the meaning of life. The object is to find out where their interests are and then ask questions to find out more. The question, "What do you think about . . ." usually leads to a person's beliefs. If you asked him about his religious background, you might follow it up with, "What do you think about your church experience now that you are away from home?" Or, "Do you now take your religious beliefs more seriously or less seriously **45** than when you were younger?" Even if your friend avoids the whole topic of religion, you can develop other areas of his interest that touch upon values, nature of man and, finally, God. Politics, history, abortion, the origin of life and the future of the earth are examples of subjects that lead into Christian themes.

The third area, seldom discussed but extremely helpful when heavy dogma has been discussed, is the area of epistemology. This answers the question, How do you know what you believe is true? This question is pretty startling for most non-Christians because they have not really thought about it. This question forces most people to admit that what they believe about the things that matter most to them is often just personal opinion. A few will point to an authority like Ayn Rand or Mohammed, and some will appeal to science or reason, but most will be caught off guard when asked how they know their beliefs are really true.

In a typical conversation, you might find that your friend believes in God, heaven but not hell, Jesus as a great teacher but not divine, and man as naturally good. He or she might think the basic problem of humanity can be solved by education or a new social order. When you ask, "How do you know?" the answer may be, "Well, it just seems to make sense." Here you can take one or more of these areas and show how Jesus provides us with authoritative information. Genuine truth, not mere opinion, is introduced.

As Christians, our authority is Jesus Christ. He is unique because he claimed to be the living, eternal God of the universe (see *Basic Christianity* by John Stott, pp. 22ff). If this claim is true, then his answers to the meaningful questions of life are of the utmost importance.

When you present your Christian belief to unbelievers, they must know who your authority is, and why you believe he is a reliable authority. I recommend the approach taken by C. S. Lewis in *Mere Christianity* and by John Stott in *Basic Christianity*: A decision must be made about the character of Jesus Christ—he is either a liar, a lunatic, a legend or the Lord. Be able to cite evidence for the historicity of the Gospel accounts of Christ's life (see *The New Testament Documents: Are They Reliable?* by F. F. Bruce and *History and Christianity* by John Warwick Montgomery). Once you have established the reasonableness of Christ's authority, you are free to talk about your friend's views on life without getting caught up in endless disagreements. In this way, your friend does not disagree with you, but with Christ. If he says, "That is just your interpretation," take him to the passage and ask him how he interprets it.

As you introduce Jesus Christ into the conversation, you will find the questions start coming your way for a change. You might select one area, such as the nature of humanity or the afterlife, and show how Jesus' teaching has something to say to it. This means you must have a good grasp of what Jesus taught and how it fits into everyday experience.

When you get to this point, your outline of the gospel or memorized version of the Christian message will prove useful to you. You can proceed to show how the life and death of Jesus mean life for us. You can speak of the nature of God, the problem of sin, what Jesus Christ has done for us and what response is required of us—how to become a Christian.

In order to avoid a purely philosophical discussion, intersperse your conversation with references to what Christ has done for you experientially and what he can do for the listener. Our God is not only rational, he is also personal. We need to make this clear, whenever we present the gospel, by speaking, not just to the mind, but to all the needs of the person.

Undoubtedly this approach can be learned and practiced without thought of the Holy Spirit's work or our need to trust God for wisdom and understanding. But without the love and compassion that come with a consistent walk with God, this approach, like any other, will be merely an academic exercise. God often draws people to himself by means of his character displayed in the lives of his children. In so doing, the listener can relate to the message of Christ as a whole person—with mind, emotions and experience.

Mark Pettersen, a graduate of Dallas Theological Seminary, served as a staff member with Inter-Varsity in Texas. He is currently pastoring a church in Emporia, Kansas.

SHARING CHRIST, OURSELVES AND PIZZA... ALL AT ONCE

BECKY MANLEY

7

Christians and non-Christians have something in common: They are both uptight about evangelism. The common fear of Christians seems to be, "How many people did I offend this week?" They think that they must offend in order to be a good evangelist. A tension begins to build inside: Should I be sensitive to people and forget about evangelism, or should I blast them with the gospel and forget about their person? Many Christians choose to be aware of the person but then feel defensive and guilty for not evangelizing. There's something wrong with this concept of evangelism.

Whenever I speak on the topic of evangelism I always sense that people are breathlessly waiting for the new, argument-proof, jelled approach, the magic formula that works on one and all or your money back. But even if I had such a formula to sell, it still would not work. Our problem in evangelism is not that we do not have enough information—it is that *we do not know how to be ourselves.* We have not grasped that it really is O.K. for us to be who we are, when we are with non-Christians, even if we do not have all the answers to their questions or if our knowledge of Scripture is limited. We forget we are called to be witnesses to what we have seen and know, not to what we do not know. The key is obedience, not a Th.D. in theology.

But there is a deeper problem here. Our uneasiness with non-Christians reflects our uneasiness with our own humanity. Because we are not certain about what it means to be human (or spiritual, for that matter), we struggle in relating naturally, humanly to the world. For example, many of us avoid evangelism for fear that we will offend someone. Yet how often have we told a non-Christian that is why we are hesitating?

I have every right to say, "Look, I'm really excited about sharing with you who God is. But I also know that I hate it when people push 'religion' on me, so if I come on too strong will you tell me?" By saying this I am communicating that we have a great deal in common: I do not want to dump the gospel, and he or she does not want to be dumped on. So on the basis of this common human bond, I am freed to share my faith.

self-discovery God has given me increased freedom to talk about him to others. But it has not always been that way. I remember reflecting on my evangelistic ministry one day as a student. It occurred to me that although I had lots of non-Christian friends, and some had become Christians through my influence, no one had ever become a Christian in my presence. As I pondered why I still felt uncomfortable about evangelism, I discovered several things about myself.

First, I was so afraid of being identified as a religious weirdo or a Jesus freak that I often remained silent when the topic of God came up. How people saw me mattered more than how God did. Ironically, most people respect and respond to a person who has definite ideas and who communicates them clearly rather than someone who seems apologetic and wishy-washy. (We have much to learn from Marxists in their boldness.)

Second, although I saw the needs and emptiness in the lives of my non-Christian friends, I could not imagine that it was Jesus Christ whom they were really searching for. Jesus was for "religious folk," not for my pagan friends. So because I never really expected them to respond to the gospel, they did not.

Third, I feared that Jesus was just "my trip." Wasn't it arrogant to suggest that *my* view was the only way? But as I grew to understand the nature of Christianity, I saw that our faith stands on historical criteria, not just subjective experience. Truth was the issue, not a feeling in my heart. God was not asking me to stand on my own ideas or emotions, but rather on the very person and work of Jesus Christ. If anyone was guilty of being offensive it was Jesus—not me. It was *his* idea that he was the only way to God, not mine. Realizing this freed me to not cower when accused of being narrow. I could **51** answer, "I know, and isn't it amazing that Jesus actually said so many narrow things? Wouldn't it be intriguing to study him to discover why he made such egotistical claims?"

Next, I was paralyzed by fear that I would offend people and forever ruin their chance of entering the kingdom. So I thought, "I'll just be nice and smile and hope they catch on." It is odd but I have noticed that offending people is rarely the problem. If you are sensitive enough to realize it can be a problem, then it is usually not your problem.

I also could not talk about God in a natural way. I was fine until the topic of "religion" came up. Suddenly I felt as if I needed to sound "spiritual," and instead of listening, I would panic because I could not remember any Scripture verses. My hands would get clammy; my eyes would dart from side to side, hoping no one else was listening; the tone of my voice would change and I would begin talking "religiously." And then I would wonder why *they* always looked so uncomfortable when we talked about spiritual things! My problem was that I did not think God could be a natural, integrated part of an ongoing discussion about movies, classes, exams or boyfriends. I did not have an integrated Christian world view; God was compartmentalized and separated from "normal" living.

And finally, no one ever became a Christian through me because I never asked tnem to! Why? Because I was petrified that if I brought someone to the point of becoming a Christian, God would not come through. That would put me in an embarrassing situation so I avoided taking the risk.

52 **unsuccessful cover-up** It was not until an

atheist friend of mine completely amazed me by becoming a Christian that I began to make some startling discoveries, based on her sharing how she had felt before accepting Christ.

"At first I thought, 'Fine, let Becky have her religion—that's her bag. I'm not the least bit interested, but if that's her thing then it's all right with me.' Then you invited me to dinner and before we ate you asked if we could thank God for the food. I thought, 'Oh, how quaint.' Only you didn't just thank him for the food—you thanked him for *me* and our friendship! It made me feel so good inside. I never thought you felt our relationship had anything to do with God. But then I thought, 'That's ridiculous—thanking someone who doesn't exist for me.'

"Then we went to the Bergman film and afterwards you said you'd studied the very same concept that was in the film in your Quiet Time that day. I never dreamed God would have anything remotely in common with modern cinema! Another day you invited me to an objective, no-strings-attached study of the person of Jesus in the Bible. Fine. Only the trouble was—I really liked the guy! He seemed so real as we would read about him each week.

"But you know what affected me most? All my life I used to think, 'How arrogant for someone to call himself a Christian, to think he's that good.' But then I got to know you—and Becky, you are far from perfect, yet you call yourself a Christian. So my first shock was to discover you 'blow it' like I do. But the biggest shock was that you admitted it, where I couldn't. Suddenly I saw that being a Christian didn't mean never failing, but admitting when you've failed. I wanted to keep Christ in a box and let you be religious during Bible studies. But the more you let me inside your life—and the more I knew the real you, with the problems and joys—the more impossible it became to keep the lid on Christianity. Even your admission of weaknesses drove me to him!"

That confession changed my life. What amazed me was that she had seen me in all kinds of circumstances—she had seen the real me—and it gave the gospel *more* power, not less. I had always thought I should cover up my doubts and problems, because if she really knew me she would not become a Christian. But the more real and transparent I was (even with my weaknesses), the more real Jesus Christ became to her.

Now please get this straight. I am not condoning sin by saying we must be human with each other. God's call is to perfection. I am not suggesting we share our weaknesses as if it's a "competitive sinning" match in order to be real. Sin is not God's brand of humanity; perfect obedience is. But so is humble confession when we fail. So our goal must be to live within the balance of aiming for perfect obedience and complete vulnerability. The paradox I constantly experience is that as I allow people inside—to see the real me with the pain and problems as well as the successes—they tell me they see God. It is when I cover up (ironically, for "God's reputation") and try to appear "together," with no problems, that they can only see Becky.

called to be human I had to learn from experience what Scripture teaches in 1 Thessalonians 2:8:
54 To share the gospel we must share our life, our real

person. If we do not grasp that Christ has freed us to be authentic, we will see evangelism as a project instead of a lifestyle. And we will tend to see non-Christians more as objects of our evangelistic efforts than as authentic persons.

I remember asking a girl once if she felt comfortable in the area of evangelism. "Oh yes!" she responded, "I do it twice a week." (Somehow it sounded more like taking her multiple vitamins.) Evangelism is not just something you "do"—out there—and then get back to "normal" living. Evangelism involves taking people seriously, getting across to their island of concerns and needs, and then sharing that Christ is Lord in the context of our natural living situations.

The problem stems, as I have said, from our great difficulty in believing that God is glorified in our utter humanity, rather than in our spiritually programmed responses. Most of us fear that who we are inside just is not enough. So we cover up our honest questions and doubts thinking they would not sound spiritual. But in doing this we forfeit our most important tool in evangelism—our real person. Not to accept our humanness means we lose our point of authentic contact with the world. We, of all people, should be offering the world a picture of what it means to be truly human. Yet it is often Christians who fear their humanity more than anyone else.

Just as there is confusion concerning what it means to be human, so is there confusion about what it means to be spiritual. We feel it is more spiritual to take our non-Christian roommate to a Bible study or to church than to a play or out for pizza. Not only do we not understand our natural points 55 of contact with the world, we do not understand our natural points of contact with God himself. He made us human beings. He is therefore interested in every aspect of our humanness. We dare not limit him to Bible studies and discussions with Christians. He created life and he desires to be glorified in the totality of all that adds up to life. And his power and presence will come crashing through to the world as we let him live fully in every aspect of our lives.

jesus, our model Do we have any models for the kind of humanity that God intended? Let's turn to the first whole human being who ever lived. The life of Jesus Christ is our objective information on what it means to be human. He told us that as the Father sent him into the world, so he is sending us. How then did the Father send him? Essentially he became one of us. The Word became flesh. God did not send a telegram, or shower evangelistic Bible study books from heaven, or drop a million bumper stickers from the sky saying, "Smile, Jesus loves you." He sent a man, his Son, to communicate the message. His strategy has not changed. He still sends men and women—before he sends tracts and techniques—to change the world. You may think his strategy is risky—but that's God's problem, not yours.

In Jesus, then, we have our model for how to relate to the world, and it's a model of vulnerability and identification. Jesus was a remarkably open man. He did not think it was unspiritual for him (fully realizing he was the Son of God) to share his physical needs (Jn. 4:7). He did not fear losing his testimony by asking for the emotional and prayerful support of friends in the Garden of Gethsemane. Here is our model for genuine godliness—and we see him asking for support and desiring others to minister to him. We must learn then to relate transparently and vulnerably to others because that is God's style of relating to us. Jesus commands us to "go" and then preach—not to preach and then leave. We are not to shout the gospel from a safe and respectable distance and remain uninvolved. We must open our lives enough to let people see that we laugh and hurt and cry too. If Jesus left all of heaven and glory to become one of us, shouldn't we at least be willing to leave our dorm room or Bible study circle to reach out to a friend?

How can we vulnerably and humanly relate to people in a way that will change the world? I think Jesus loved and changed the world in two ways: by his radical identification with men and women, and by his radical difference. Jesus seemed to respond to people first by noticing what they had in common (Jn. 4:7). But it was often in the context of their similarities that Jesus' difference came crashing through (Jn. 4:10). It was as people discovered his profound humanness that they began to recognize his deity. God's holiness became shattering and penetrating as Jesus confronted people on his very own level of humanity. But the point is that it took both, his radical identification and his radical difference, to change the world. So it will be for us.

collected clues What can we do then, to relate authentically to the world and change it as Jesus did? If you are wanting to make contact with people around you as a representative of Jesus Christ, here are some collected clues that may help.

1/*Be yourself—plus.* Let God make you fully you. Rejoice in your God-given temperament, and use it for God's purposes. God made some of us shy, others outgoing. We should praise him for that. If you are shy, remember that your shyness is not an excuse to avoid relationships—rather it is a means to love the world in a different way than an extrovert.

I get discouraged when I hear people say that it is easy for me to evangelize because I am outgoing. Being an extrovert *is not* the essential tool in evangelism—obedience and love are. There are many people I could never reach, and would probably only intimidate, because I am outgoing. God will have to use other Christians to reach them. But I do not feel guilty about it because I have learned that God is not glorified in my life with my roommate's personality. I must be who I am created to be. And I must reach out to others in a way that is both sensitive to the person with whom I am talking and *consistent* with my own personality.

But regardless of our temperaments, we all must become initiators. More and more I see that the mark of mature Christians is whether they choose to be the "hosts" or the "guests" in relationships. Christians must be the ones who love, care and listen first. We can all take initiative, whether in a quiet or more conspicuous way.

2/*Be a risk-taker.* To take initiative opens us up to the risk of rejection. To let people inside our lives is a frightening but essential ingredient in evangelism. It is also a risk to leave our security blankets in order to penetrate *their* lives.

Recently I was walking through O'Hare Airport **58** in Chicago when my purse slipped and everything tumbled out. As I was stuffing things back inside, a young woman with a baby stopped to ask the time. Then she nervously bit her lip and asked, "You don't know where I could get a drink, do you?" I didn't. But as I searched her face, I saw that she was distraught. So I stood up and began initiating a conversation. She quickly interrupted with, "Do you know how much a drink would cost here?" I could see we were getting nowhere, and suddenly I heard myself saying, "Gee, I don't know, but would you like me to go with you to find the bar?" "Oh, would you? I would really love the company," she responded.

Off we went in search of a bar. And all the way I was kicking myself for it—going to a bar at noon with a perfect stranger. How unorthodox! Then I thought, "I wonder what Jesus would do in a situation like this?" I realized that he would probably be more concerned about *why* she needed the drink than about going into a bar. I knew that if I could not be at ease around her when she had a drink in her hand, and allow God to lead me into what *he* perceived as a mission field, then I would not be very effective in communicating God's unconditional love.

After we found the bar it took only minutes before she began sharing that she had decided to leave her husband. Her husband, unaware of her decision, would be meeting her at the airport in Michigan. She was petrified at facing his response and felt totally alone. "Oh, but it's ridiculous telling this to a complete stranger—how boring this must be for you," she would comment and then talk on.

The saddest part was her obvious inability to believe anyone could care for her. She trusted no one. **59**

When at one point she mentioned a problem with which I told her I could identify, she said, "Oh, so *that's* why you act as if you care. Listen, aren't you afraid of picking up strangers like me? You really should be more careful." As I began to tell her who God was and that he was the one who brought me into situations like this, she seemed to hang on every word.

Soon we were walking to her plane, but I felt torn inside. I wanted to reach out to her and tell her how moved I was by her problems, and that there was a God who cared deeply for her. But she was so cold and defensive that I feared her rejection. Finally at the gate I took her hand and said, "Listen, I want you to know that I really care about you, and I'll be praying for you the minute you get off the plane." She just stared blankly at me. Then, turning away, she said, "Um . . . I'm sorry—I just don't know how to handle love," and walked away.

The encounter was not a smashing success, but I felt I was obedient. Being a Christian means taking risks: risking that our love will be rejected, misunderstood or even ignored. Now I am not suggesting that you race to your local bar for Jesus. But if you find yourself in a situation in which you believe God has put you, then accept the risk for his love's sake.

3/*See beneath the crust.* Once we have taken the risk and are in contact with a person, we must never assume that he or she won't be open to Christianity. Once we get beneath the surface of a person we will usually discover a sea of needs. We must learn how to interpret those needs correctly, as Jesus did. Jesus was not turned off by needs—even needs wrongly met—because they told him something about the person.

The Samaritan woman had had five husbands and was currently living with a sixth man. The disciples took one look at her and felt, "That woman? Become a Christian? No way, why just look at her lifestyle!" But Jesus looked at the very same lifestyle and came to the opposite conclusion. What Jesus saw in her frantic male-hopping was not just a loose woman. It was not her human need for tenderness that alarmed Jesus, but rather the way she sought to meet that need. Even more, Jesus saw that her need indicated a real hunger for God. He seemed to be saying to the disciples, "Look at what potential she has for God—see how hard she's trying to find the right thing in all the wrong places."

That blows the lid right off evangelism for me. How many Samaritan men and women do you know? Everywhere I am, I see people frantically looking for the right things in all the wrong places. The tragedy is that so often my initial response is to withdraw and assume they will never become Christians. Yet God has shown me that they are usually the ones who are most open. We must ask ourselves: "How do I interpret the needs and lifestyles of my friends? Do I look at their drinking or sleeping around or radical politics and say, 'That's wrong' and walk away? Or do I penetrate their mask and discover why they do this in the first place? And then do I try to love them where they are?"

We can show people that they are right to want to fill the void, and then they may be surprised by joy to discover that the emptiness inside is a "God-shaped vacuum."

4/*Avoid the "Holy Huddle Syndrome."* We must not become, as John Stott puts it, "rabbit-hole Christians." You know—the kind who pops his head out of the hole, leaves his Christian roommate in the morning and scurries to class, only to frantically search for a Christian to sit next to (an odd way to approach a mission field). Thus he proceeds from class to class. When dinner time comes, he sits with all the Christians in his dorm at one huge table and thinks, "What a witness." From there he goes to his all-Christian Bible study, and he might even catch a prayer meeting where the Christians pray for the non-believers on his floor. (But what luck that he was able to live on the only floor with seventeen Christians!) Then at night he scurries back to his Christian roommate. Safe! He made it through the day and his only contacts with the world were those mad, brave dashes to and from Christian activities.

What an insidious reversal of the biblical command to be "salt" and "light" to the world. The "rabbit-hole Christian" remains insulated and isolated from the world when he is commanded to penetrate it. How can we be the salt of the earth if we never get out of the saltshaker?

Christians, however, are not the only ones to blame for this phenomenon. The tragedy is that even the world encourages our isolationism. Have you ever wondered why everyone always "behaves" when the minister joins the group on a television talk show? Suddenly their language changes and their behavior improves. Why? They want to do their part to keep the Reverend feeling holy. They will play the religious game while he is around because he needs to be protected from that cold, real world out there.

Sometimes non-Christians will act oddly around us because they are genuinely convicted by the Holy

Spirit in us—and that is good. But all too often they are behaving "differently" because they feel that is the way they are *supposed* to act around religious types.

I am often put in "religious boxes" when people discover what my profession is. Because I travel a great deal, I have a "clergy card" which enables me sometimes to travel at reduced rates. The only problem is that no one will ever believe I am authorized to use it! Somehow a young female just is not what the airline ticket agents have in mind when they see a clergy card. More than once I have been asked, "Okay, honey, now where did you rip this off?"

The funniest case occurred when I was flying from San Francisco to Portland. I arrived at the counter and was greeted by an exceedingly friendly male ticket agent.

"Well, hel-lo-o-o there!" he said.

"Ah . . . I'd like to pick up my ticket to Portland, please."

"Gee, I'm sorry—you won't be able to fly there tonight."

"Why—is the flight canceled?"

"No, it's because you're going out with me tonight."

"What?"

"Listen, I know this great restaurant with a hot band. You'll never regret it."

"Oh, I'm sorry, I really must get to Portland. Do you have my ticket?"

"Aw, what's the rush? I'll pick you up at 8:00. . . ."

"Look, I really must go to Portland," I said.

"Well, okay. Too bad though. Hey, I can't find your ticket. Looks like it's a date then!"

"Oh, I forgot to tell you, it's a . . . special ticket," I said.

"Oh, is it youth fare?"

"No, um, well, it's . . . ah, *clergy*," I whispered as I leaned over the counter.

He froze. "What did you say?"

"It's clergy."

"CLERGY!?!" he yelled, as the entire airport looked our way. His face went absolutely pale, and you could tell he was horrified by only one thought, "Oh no, I flirted with that nun!"

When he disappeared behind the counter, I could hear him whisper to the other ticket agent a few feet away, "Hey George, get a load of that girl up there, she's *clergy*." Suddenly another man rose from behind the counter, smiled and nodded and disappeared again. Now I do not think I have ever felt so religious in my entire life. As I stood there trying to look as secular as possible, my ticket agent reappeared and stood back several feet behind the desk. Looking a bit shaken and sounding like a confused tape recording he said, "Good afternoon. We certainly hope there have been no inconveniences. And on behalf of Hughes Airwest, we'd like to wish you a very safe and pleasant flight . . . Sister Manley."

As humorous as this incident was, I think it shows how difficult it is to maintain our authenticity before the world. The challenge is to not allow ourselves to become more or less than human.

5/*Christians are positive!* Our attitude in responding to people is crucial. If you notice that non-Christians seem embarrassed, apologetic and defensive, it is probably because they are picking up *your* attitude. If you assume they will be absolutely fascinated to discover the true nature of Christianity, they probably will. If you communicate enthusiasm, not defensiveness, and carefully listen instead of sounding like a recording of "Answers to Questions You Didn't Happen to Ask," non-Christians will become intrigued. Learn to delight in all their questions—especially the ones you cannot answer. I often tell people I am very grateful that God is using them to sharpen me intellectually when I am stumped by a question. I tell them I do not know the answer but I can't wait to investigate it.

Learn also to identify with their defenses against Christianity. When talking with an intellectual professor, for example, we have every right to say, "I think one of the hardest issues a Christian must face is how in the world we know that it's true. Are we deluding ourselves and worshiping on the basis of need rather than truth?" In that way we can free non-Christians to feel at home with us. Walls are torn down and bridges built when *we* suggest the objections they may have.

Finally, approach relationships with non-Christians looking for ways in which God made you alike. Paul looked for points he had in common with others and began building from there (see Acts 17:22). An experience I had last year illustrates this point.

The girl who lives below me in my apartment house is a real swinger. She had just moved in, and every time I saw her she would be on her way to another party. We always exchanged friendly words and one day she said, "Becky, I like you. You're all right. Let's get together next week and smoke a joint, okay?" I replied, "Gee, thanks! I really like you too and I'd love to spend time with you. Actually I can't stand the stuff, but I'd sure love to do something else. See you later!"

Of course she looked a bit surprised, not so much because I did not smoke grass, but because I had expressed real appreciation at the thought of spending time with her. I could have told her "I'm a Christian and I never touch the stuff," but I wanted to affirm whatever I possibly could first, without selling short the standards of a Christian. Too often we broadcast what we "don't do" when we should be trying to discover genuine points of contact.

6/*Put it all together.* First, investigate. We need to learn how to be listeners first and proclaimers second. It is like rowing around an island, carefully studying the shoreline for an appropriate landing place. We explore our non-Christian friends' religious and family backgrounds, cultural interests, needs, dreams and fears. It is amazing to me that we spend fortunes so that missionaries can learn foreign languages while it never occurs to us that we must "learn the language" of our friends at home. We must get inside their thought forms and understand their questions. Don't leap to resolve every question; raise some! (God does that all the time in Scripture.)

Next, stimulate. Once we have some idea of who we are talking to, we must learn to arouse their curiosity about the gospel. I think this is one of the most neglected aspects of evangelism. We try to saturate people with the light before we have caught their attention. In Acts 26:18 Paul says he was called *first* to open their eyes, *before* he helped them turn from darkness to light. He was called to arouse their interest so they would want to hear his message. We must learn to be "fishers of men" and not "hunters of men." We need to look at Paul and Jesus to study their "fishing techniques."

Jesus was often deliberately vague and intriguing to people at first, not giving the whole answer until he had their complete interest. He knew that the Samaritan woman would not have a clue about what "living water" meant, any more than Nicodemus would comprehend the term "born again." He was deliberately obscure to see if they had any spiritual interest and, if so, to enhance it.

Paul aroused the curiosity of the Thessalonian Jews in the synagogue with his fierce logic and rational arguments. At Areopagus he captured the interest of the Greeks with his ability to use their secular poets to affirm his points. We too must develop a style of "intriguing" evangelism—not only through our conversation, but in our love for each other, our personal godliness and our genuine concern for non-Christians.

Finally, relate. Once we have discovered where people are and have aroused their interest in what we have to say, we are ready to relate the gospel message. Steps one and two are the necessary pre-evangelistic steps that will enable us to communicate Christ more effectively. But it is not enough to take the first two steps without the third. Paul, for example, knew his audience, found where they needed to grapple with commitment and then proclaimed the gospel (Acts 17:16-34).

Notice that Paul's message contained content and not just experience. Somehow it is difficult to imagine St. Paul on top of Areopagus defending his faith before secular philosophers by saying, "Gee, I dunno fellas, it's just this feeling in my heart." Our conversion experience may illustrate the power of the gospel, but it does not explain it. I cringe sometimes at the lack of content I hear when students are sharing their faith. Jesus begins to sound more like a "happy pill" to be popped or a trip to beat all trips than a Lord to be obeyed at any cost.

fully human We have discussed how we can identify with the world as Jesus did. But Jesus also changed the world by his radical difference. How will our radical difference be expressed? The tension lies between identifying with the world and loving it as deeply as Jesus did (being similar to the world), and yet obeying the command "be ye therefore perfect" (being different from the world). We must remember that identification with the world does not equal being identical with the world. If we seek to understand the world but live exactly as non-Christians do, no impact will be made. Only as we identify with the world while living supernatural lives will revolution take place. That means our daily time alone with God will be critical to our evangelism, for it will change us into the likeness of Christ. Persistent prayer is equally vital—we must learn to love our friends enough to pray daily for them.

But I think our most radical difference will be felt when we live as we were created to be—fully human. Jesus has shown us that the most essential ingredient of true humanity is the freedom to respond totally, completely and passionately to God. If we let God make us authentic humans—not subcultural Christians, but affirming, vulnerable, open people who penetrate the world and love it as deeply as Jesus did—then the presence of God will be overwhelmingly felt by the world.

I sometimes wonder if we have really grasped

who we are and what we have to offer. We are a new race! A race of people who have become authentically human through Jesus Christ. The very enfleshment of God dwells in us. He reaches out, touches and loves the world through us.

It cost God everything to identify with the nature of mankind. So will it cost us a great deal to identify with the nature of non-Christians. To give the message is easy. To give our lives is costly. But it is the giving of our lives that changes the world, for it authenticates the message that we preach. God asks for nothing less.

Becky Manley serves on Inter-Varsity staff in Oregon and Washington.

CAMPUS CASUALTY: A CASE STUDY
C. STEPHEN BOARD

8

Mike hit campus two years ago as your usual confident atheist. He had a warm, atheistic home life. He was trained in an atheist high school, armed with the atheist catechism. But Mike lost his faith in college.

Things began to get wobbly right away during freshman orientation. Mike met his roommate who turned out to be one of those religious people. Wilf, the roommate, got things going by moving in a Bible, a catchy religious poster, and a big box of theological books.

"I've heard about people like you," Wilf said. "But I've never met one. Maybe you can explain your beliefs to me sometime."

That night, while Wilf was away, Mike reviewed his techniques in a book he had brought, *How to Give Away Your Unbelief.* It dealt with answering religious people's questions, getting conversations going, what to do when a religious person wants to say a prayer before a meal—that sort of thing.

It was kind of funny, the way Mike and Wilf swapped propaganda. Mike gave Wilf a copy of *The God Who Is Not There*, and Wilf gave Mike a copy of *Why I Am Not an Atheist.*

In class the pressure was really on. Mike never felt more uncomfortable as an atheist. Back in atheist high, he had learned a pack of arguments for the nonexistence of God. Science, he had learned, supported materialism. Literature supported secularism. Psychology dissolved all your beliefs into conditioning. But here at college Mike learned how parochial an atheistic high school can be.

Zoology, for example. The zo prof got loads of mileage out of the design of animal life on earth, right down to the genetic chemistry. "I'll bet some of you have the childish idea that all this just happened," the prof chortled. Seemed like the whole class cracked up in horse laughs. "Now that you are at the university you may as well grow up. Part of your education is in learning reasons for things and not copping out with explanations like 'chance.' " Mike was glad when the semester ended.

In literature Mike felt safe. He had memorized a few poems of unbelief and had read some profound atheistic novels back in high school. William Ernest Henley's "Invictus" was one of his favorites. But freshmen introductory lit revised everything. Mike's assigned research project was a comparison of John Donne and Gerard Manley Hopkins, two poets who believed in you-know-Who. His paper was charged, so to speak, with the grandeur of God.

Prose was not much better. God lurked everywhere, from readings in the Bible, St. Augustine, Samuel Johnson and Tolstoy, to Dostoevsky.

The same story in history. He had always thought an atheist ruler would be more enlightened and humane than one who believed in God or gods. That seemed to make sense as they studied the Inquisition and the religious wars. But the twentieth century shot the theory to pieces: all that bloodshed under atheistic dictators.

At the end of his freshman year, our hero was ready to drop out of university and transfer to a private atheistic college. The year had worn him down. "My God, what's happening to me?" he mumbled, as he crossed the quad to avoid an outdoor rally promoting the reality of God.

The summer helped him recover; home with the folks, the old friends, the familiar home town with its familiar disbelief in God. True, some of those people bugged him. The family Atheist Advisor was a hypocrite, and Mike's own atheistic parents were not all they ought to be. But by the end of the summer, he felt up to another year at the U.

Well, sometime that winter, between Christmas and the Day of the Rising Son (that's what people on campus were calling Easter), Mike went over to the Other Side, joined the God people and installed a sky in his world.

It seems his doubts about atheism had increased for months before he finally packed it all in.

His psych classes had taught him to criticize his beliefs. "I'm a child of atheist parents and the product of an atheist background; I've never thought it through for myself." Another thing that bothered him was, "What about all the people who have never heard of atheism? They seem to get along O.K. without changing their beliefs." But the big thing was the problem of evil. "What about all the suffering in the world? If there is no God, injustice will never be put right—it just goes on and on, evil heaped on evil and never judged."

Mike wrote a letter describing his conversion to a high-school friend. "It was like the sun coming out," he wrote. "I could see God make sense here at school the more I thought about him. I feel like I've grown up . . . or maybe just been born."

African Bantu proverb: "He who never travels thinks mother is the only cook." What hazards await easy unbelief on campus this year. Or next.

C. Stephen Board is executive editor of Eternity *magazine. He was formerly on Inter-Varsity staff in Chicago and editor of* HIS *magazine.*

ENCOURAGING
A DECISION
PAUL E. LITTLE

9

How can you tell when a person is ready to accept Christ? The simplest answer is—ask.

But this does not really solve the problem. We still have trouble knowing *how* to ask a person. I have found it helpful to ask this question, "Have you ever personally trusted Christ or are you still on the way?" This sufficiently defines what a Christian is so that the average person will not say Yes unless he or she knows what you mean. If the person asks what you mean, that may be a tip-off that he isn't a believer. In any case you have the opportunity to explain the gospel. Most often the response is, "That's me, I'm still on the way." Then the second question could be, "That's interesting. How far along the way are you?" Without the slightest inhibition or embarrassment the person can tell you how far along the road of spiritual pilgrimage he or she is (or isn't). Your friend may not even believe Jesus Christ existed in history. He could have a very distorted idea of Christ, thinking of him only as a great philosopher or teacher. Or he may know the gospel better than you do. In this case the problem is not lack of information, but a failure to respond to the information he or she already has.

objections A person may raise various objections to becoming a Christian. Some may be important and others insignificant. The person may say, for instance, that he or she doesn't know enough. We need to help that person see it is not a question of how much is known, but whether he believes what he does know and is willing to respond to it. A person never fully understands the gospel. If we wait until we fully understand we will never trust Christ.

Sometimes a person will say, "I am not good enough." Help him or her see that is exactly the kind of person Christ died for.

Frequently a person will say, "I don't think I could last and I don't want to be a hypocrite." But it is not a question of holding on to Christ and hoping that your grip will not fail. Rather, Christ grasps hold of you. He has said that he gives his sheep eternal life, they shall never perish and no one can pluck them out of his hand (Jn. 10:28).

It is important to avoid two extremes. The one is precipitation. We tend to push people into decisions they are not prepared for, either because they do not understand or they are being pressured against their will. This is wrong. The other extreme is procrastination—letting people put the decision off as though it were not very important. Help them see that the issue is a matter of life and death that demands commitment, since no one has the guarantee of tomorrow morning's sunrise.

When someone indicates that he or she would like to receive Christ, explain exactly what is involved in becoming a Christian and then ask the person to explain it back to you. If your friend can give you back (in reasonably recognizable form) the essence of what you have told him, then very likely he has heard and understood you correctly.

In helping a person make a decision we must state clearly that there is something to be believed and someone to be received. In order to be a Christian a person must believe certain things about Christ's deity, life, death and resurrection, and about his diagnosis of our sinful condition. Mere intellectual assent to those facts does not make a person a Christian. The person must receive Christ into his or her life and become a child of God. It is the same in marriage. Belief in the other person does not make us married. We must respond with our will in order to establish a relationship. In becoming a Christian we believe in a person and then receive him into our lives. Only then can we say we have a relationship with God. John 1:12 explains this.

Revelation 3:20 can help a person understand this. I often say, "Suppose someone came to the door of your home and knocked. How would you let the knocking person inside?" The person thinks for a moment and says, "I would open the door." After agreeing with that, I say, "And then what would you do?" Usually a smile breaks across his face and he says, "I would invite the person to come in." This is exactly how you become a Christian. Christ is knocking at the door of your life. He wants to come in, but he will never force his way in or gate-crash. Instead, the moment you invite him to come in, he will. This is the point of the prayer that we make to receive him.

prayer If the person definitely wants to receive Christ and seems to understand what is involved, you might suggest several options about praying to receive Christ. Since he or she might not be accustomed to praying, you can offer to pray a prayer which can be repeated after you phrase by phrase. After saying what your prayer will include, emphasize the fact that the words themselves have no magic. Unless they represent what your friend really feels in his heart, they do not mean anything. The person may want to pray silently, so you should offer that option.

If a person I am talking with selects that option, I always ask him to tell me, after he has prayed silently and I have prayed audibly, what he said to God. Frequently, he will have thanked God for the birds and the bees and the sunset. I then ask him if he really spoke to Jesus Christ to thank him for dying for his sins and to invite him into his life as Lord and master. He will frequently say, "I guess not." I agree with him and suggest that he pray again, addressing himself to the Lord in those terms. Sometimes a person prefers to go back to his room and pray. If he does, I urge him to call me or see me within twenty-four hours to tell me the decision that he has made.

help Having helped a person over the line, you need to give some immediate help. Help him or her to see that the assurance of salvation rests on what Christ has done on the cross and on the promise of the Word of God. It does not depend on how he or she feels at the moment. Some people feel tremendously relieved at conversion. Others have little feeling at all. This varies with the individual. The fact of Christ and the faith a person places in him, not the feeling, are the guide.

New Christians need some help to begin reading the Word of God for themselves to take in spiritual food. It is usually helpful to suggest a specific passage, like the beginning of the Gospel of Mark. Suggest that they ask one question of the text as they read, such as "What does this teach me about Christ?" or "Is there a command I should obey or an example to follow?" They may also need help in relationships with both non-Christian friends and family. It is important to share this new faith with family, but this can be very difficult.

If a new Christian goes home and immediately judges his or her family as non-Christian, they will probably deeply resent this new faith. He or she might do better to assume that they understand the facts of the gospel too, and tell them this. But the new Christian should also say that these facts have suddenly become alive and meaningful. This is why he wants to share with them what has happened.

If non-Christian friends are going to sweep the new Christian into an old life of sin, it would be best to break with them. For the most part, however, they will be best able to see how being a Christian has changed their friend. They present prime opportunities for witness. The new Christian may well be dropped by old friends, but he or she should not drop them, except in extreme cases where these friends would drag the new Christian down.

Scripture teaches us that God wants to use us in reaping as well as in sowing and watering. Many more of us would have the privilege of being the last link in the chain if we "popped the question" to more people than we do. Take time right now to think about your circle of friends. Is there someone who is waiting to be asked? If you were to approach that person in love, could you help him or her make a specific decision for Christ?

Paul E. Little, author of How to Give Away Your Faith, *served on Inter-Varsity staff from 1950 until his death in 1975. He was also Associate Professor of Evangelism at Trinity Evangelical Divinity School.*

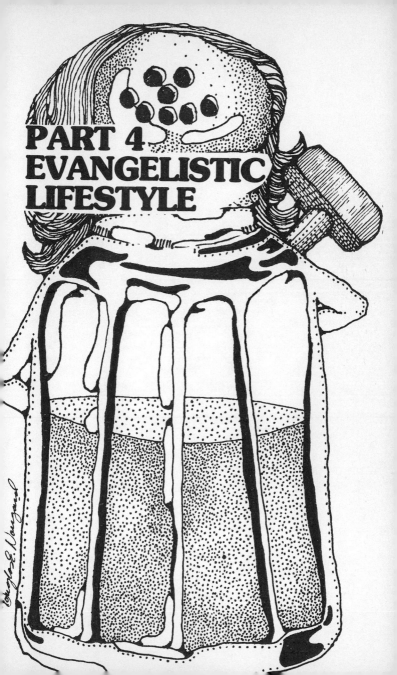

PART 4
EVANGELISTIC
LIFESTYLE

HOW TO DEVELOP AN EVANGELISTIC LIFESTYLE
TERRELL SMITH

10

Does evangelism fit in your life like the sections in *Time* magazine? *Time* has a section for economics, for the world, for sports, for education and for religion. Nothing actually ties or integrates these different sections with each other, except the cover and the staples.

A Christian's life can be like that, consisting of different sections to put things into, with little integration between the sections.

We often think about evangelism as a section of life that does not fit in too well with other sections such as our education or job. Unless it fits into the religion pages of a Christian's life, it is not appropriate. Evangelism becomes something *done* at a particular time, but not at a time set aside for something else like sports. We try to turn it on and off like a light bulb. Jesus said, "You are the light of the world," and the answer we give is, "Yes, if and when I decide to be. I'll be the salt of the earth every Saturday because that's my day off." This is nonsense. Evangelism, if it is to be biblical, must be a lifestyle. It must be not a moment here and there, but a whole way of life.

In 2 Corinthians, from chapters 4 through 6, Paul gives a definition of evangelism. In short, evangelism is an honest, open statement of the truth (4:2) that Jesus is Lord (4:5), given in the power of God (4:7), to please him (5:9), controlled by the love of Christ (5:14), to persuade people (5:11), through love (6:11), to be reconciled to God (5:20). The word *evangelize* means to proclaim the gospel or to spread the good news.

what it isn't   There are four things that evangelism is not. First of all, evangelism is *not defined by positive response*. The essence of our role in evangelism is not to make converts—that is God's work. Our job is to faithfully proclaim the message. God's job is to do convicting and regeneration, to bring those spiritually dead into new life. Christians are to spread God's commandment to repent, to warn of judgment and to tell of God's sure salvation through Jesus Christ's death and resurrection (Acts 17:30-31).

When Paul preached in Athens (Acts 17) he received many different responses. Some mocked him, saying, "This guy is crazy." Other people said, "Very interesting, we'll hear you again sometime." And there was a third group of people who joined Paul—they believed.

When evangelizing, we should expect different kinds of responses. It cannot be said that Paul was not doing evangelism because some mocked him or because some didn't believe. If people laugh at us and say, "You're really off base," we dare not say that we therefore have not been doing evangelism. It may be fair to ask whether our evangelism is biblical if we see no fruit. But evangelism is not defined in terms of converts.

Second, evangelism is *not deceitful*. Paul said, in 1 Thessalonians 2:3, "Our appeal does not spring from error or uncleanness, nor is it made with guile." And he also said, "We have renounced disgraceful, underhanded ways; we refuse to practice cunning" (2 Cor. 4:2).

I wonder how many Christians, myself included, are guilty of inviting non-Christian friends to a Christian meeting where the gospel is going to be preached, but somehow conveniently forgetting to tell them that? Once they're there and a captive audience, the gospel is dumped on them.

Are we guilty of tricking people by sponsoring a lecture on some topic and giving it such a vague name that nobody is ever going to figure out that it is Christian until they have been sucked into it? Or do we approach people under some other pretense when our real intention is to confront them with a holy God who loves them? God does not need these little tricks. He doesn't need anyone to lure people along and then grab them when they can't get away. God works in people's hearts. When we are honest, when we are open, God will draw people to himself.

Third, evangelism is *not distorted*. We need to share the truth and nothing but the truth. Do we tamper with God's Word to make it more attractive, **85** leaving out "little things" which will make it more palatable, such "things" as turning and forsaking sin, repentance? Individuals need to repent. We soft sell or perhaps do not even mention at all that Jesus is Lord and that he demands to be followed as Master, as Lord, as King. To tell people that becoming a Christian means all your troubles will evaporate is a lie. (If it is true, there were not any Christians in the New Testament.)

I heard of a girl who believed that in order to present a clear picture of being a Christian she had to live a perfect, sparkling life before her roommate. She did it. She never let this roommate know that she had any problems or was struggling with anything. Her roommate eventually became a Christian and two weeks later committed suicide. She couldn't stand it. Her life still had problems which did not evaporate at conversion.

Fourth, evangelism is *not optional*. It is not for some spiritual elite. It is true that God has selected certain people in the church and given them gifts in evangelism. Jesus said, "Go therefore and make disciples of all nations . . . teaching them to observe all that I have commanded you" (Mt. 28:19-20). One of his commandments was to "go" and so that applies to *all* Christians. Failure to tell people is not just being lazy, but being disobedient to Jesus' clear command.

A look at the life of Jesus reveals that everything he did had something to do with pleasing God in evangelism. For Peter, Paul and all the other disciples, evangelism was a way of life. It was not just something they did for a couple of hours some afternoon. Why is it not a way of life for us as it should

what it is Let's consider four things a person needs to do in order to be useful to God in evangelism. First, the believer needs to *learn to love God*. Building a love relationship with God is much the same as building a love relationship with anyone else. When introduced to a person, you start getting to know him or her by spending time talking and sharing. You find out his or her likes and dislikes. As love grows, it includes doing things for the other person to please that person.

This is also true of your relationship with God. After the introduction comes time to learn to love him by spending time with him, talking with him and letting him talk to you. Prayer and Bible study accomplish this. As you discover how God loves you and what he wants from you and for you, the love relationship will grow deeper. Believers can show an appropriate love response by obeying his commandments—doing the things that please him. Jesus said, "He who has my commandments and keeps them, he it is who loves me; and he who loves me will be loved by my Father, and I will love him and manifest myself to him" (Jn. 14:21).

Second, the believer needs to *learn to love people*. Some people are less lovable than others. How do we learn to love the people we work with, the unlikeable people, people who are annoying or take our time? We need to realize their condition, their need. Remember that nonbelievers are lost, spiritually dead, separated from the Source of life. "How are men to call upon him in whom they have not believed? How are they to believe in him of whom they have not heard? And how are they to hear without a preacher? . . . So faith comes from what is heard, and what is heard comes by the **87** preaching of Christ" (Rom. 10:14, 17). Another verse teaches, "And there is salvation in no one else, for there is no other name under heaven given among men by which we must be saved" (Acts 4:12). We are given no assurance to believe that a person who dies without hearing of Christ has any hope of salvation. That is a hard thought, but God said to Ezekiel, "I have made you a watchman for the house of Israel; . . . give them warning from me. . . . (If) you give him no warning, . . . that wicked man shall die in his iniquity; but his blood I will require at your hand" (Ezek. 3:17-18). We should speak to those who are perishing. As Christians get hold of this fact, it will help us understand what it means to love other people.

Then, too, we need to *be where the people are*. Christians easily disengage themselves from much of non-Christian society. We dig our foxholes of fellowship so deep that we become like soldiers who have lost contact with the enemy. People have needs to be listened to, to be spoken to. Beneath the veneer of party, self-confidence, brains, kindness, happy-all-the-time, there is a real person: morally confused, socially dependent, religiously ignorant and spiritually dead. Someone who comes to people in openness, in love and in understanding is welcome.

Listen to people. When someone shares a problem, a glib "I'll pray for you" will not do. Dropping a little spiritual bombshell that hints of Christian commitment and hoping the person will think about it is not realistic. Ask that person, "How can I help you in this?" He or she needs prayer, and we need to get involved in his or her life.

This is what love is. Love is not gooey sentiment;

love is godly service. Jesus said, "As the Father has sent me, even so I send you" (Jn. 20:21). Jesus left his home in heaven and came to rub shoulders with publicans and sinners like us. Christians too have been sent by him. We need to leave our little Christian ghetto and rub shoulders with people.

Third, the believer needs to *get his message clear.* It is great to know God and be where the people are. But something else is needed to do evangelism—a message. What is it we are supposed to tell somebody, anyway? If a Christian spends all his time knowing God, he may know God's truth but miss the target when attempting to apply it. If a Christian spends all his time with people, he won't have any truth to tell them. We need to know God and we need to know people—then we need to learn how to apply God's truth to people's lives.

A study of the sermons in Acts or of Jesus' encounters with people reveals much. Diagram them and write down the facts they cover and the ways Jesus and the apostles worked. These sermons explain truth about God's character, how people willfully disobeyed God and how the apostles or Jesus helped them see that. The facts about the person of Christ, his life, his death, his resurrection, need to be told. People must know that they need to respond to these facts, by turning and forsaking their sin, and by placing confidence in the Lord.

As we grow in loving God, in loving people and in knowing the message, there is one more thing. The Christian has to *expect to be used* by God in evangelism. Plan for evangelism to happen in your life.

How do you plan? Pray, and in your prayers ask God for opportunities. Then you have every reason **89** to expect God to open doors and give you conversations.

Someone who gets engaged is excited about it, and eagerly tells others about the new commitment to the beloved one. No one suddenly says to himself, "I have decided that I am going to be excited about my fiancé." But I have known people who have done that same thing in evangelism.

It often happens at a conference. A speaker challenges the group about evangelism, and each enthusiastically says, "From now on, I'm going to be an excited evangelist. I'm going to go out and win the world." It does not last. It is like the time when as a little kid you got a helium balloon. You brought it home and let it go. It floated up to the ceiling and stayed there for a couple of days. Then one day it was lying on the floor all wrinkled. That is what happens to Christians who inflate themselves with evangelistic zeal. It does not work long and pretty soon all the zeal seeps out. Excitement grows naturally as love for God and love for people grow.

It is easier to have opportunities to evangelize when you are visibly Christian. Little things count—wearing a symbol or a button, placing a small New Testament on your desk in the dorm or at work. You might ask others to join you in a Bible study over your lunch break. Also, associating with other Christians and caring for their needs demonstrates the love of believers for each other. Jesus said, "By this all men will know that you are my disciples, if you have love for one another" (Jn. 13:35). There is something that draws people to Jesus Christ when they see the love going on between Christians.

if you are ready for them. For instance, when my roommate went to interview for a job at a food store he mentioned to the interviewer that he was a Christian. The interviewer then told others who worked there. The door was opened for him even before he began the job.

With a little thought and prayer, witnessing situations can be created. In a conversation ask questions like, "What are your goals in life?" instead of just, "What's your major?" There are many questions which can lead to a discussion of spiritual things. It might be helpful to share different things from your own life which can include your faith in Jesus Christ. In class Monday you might say to someone, "Last Saturday I had an interesting experience; I was at this Christian Life Seminar." And that might get a discussion going. If people know you are a Christian, they'll be watching you, and opportunities will open.

Sometimes Christians think they can witness without saying anything. On a summer job I had when I was in college I decided I would witness silently. While the other guys were telling dirty jokes during lunch hour I went off and read my Bible. As a consequence, I never had one significant conversation with anyone. I never let the other guys know why it was that I acted differently.

At times Christians must be silent verbally, but in order for witness to be effective, people must know that we are Christians. Otherwise, a Christian might live this great, good life and no one would know why. I have a friend who is not a Christian but his wife is. She cannot say too much to him because he gets angry. But you see he knows that she is a Christian. And so by her life she can be visible. **91**

Though silent verbally, her life speaks loudly.

On the first day of my freshman year at college as I was unpacking my books, including my Bible, a great opportunity appeared. I laid my Bible down on my desk. My new roommate saw it and said, "You're not some kind of a Christian, are you?" Actually he used words a little stronger than that. I was not sure how to answer because of the words he used. But just because I took my Bible out and laid it there I was visible. And because he knew that I was a Christian he was able to watch me.

Amazingly, he talked to other guys. In my dorm there were two hundred guys. Guys I had never seen before would stop me and say, "Hey, I hear you're some kind of religious person. Tell me about it." My non-Christian roommate opened many doors for me just because of that Bible I unpacked.

Eloquence should not be a concern. Einstein once remarked that if you are out to describe the truth, you should leave the eloquence to the tailor. Very often a shy person, an uneducated person or someone who just does not know how to say things with the right grammar or syntax can be very convincing because he speaks from his heart. Even though he does not tell it gracefully, he speaks with such naturalness that everyone knows he is telling the truth.

This is not a simple method to make evangelism become a way of life because one does not exist. For evangelism to become a way of life, a Christian needs to grow. Healthy evangelism comes out of healthy relationships, with God and with people. We are Christians today because the church of the first century was obedient to the Holy Spirit's prompting and went into the world, making disciples of the nations. It was over nineteen hundred years ago that Jesus gave the Great Commission. The task he set before us is not yet completed. Will evangelism be just a moment for you? Or a lifestyle?

Terrell Smith is a staff member with Inter-Varsity in Wisconsin. He first wrote for HIS *magazine as an undergraduate at the University of California, Berkeley.*

FRIENDSHIP EVANGELISM
PAUL TOKUNAGA

11

I had waited with great anticipation for this dinner engagement for many weeks. In my mind the scenario was set. I knew what I wanted to see happen. Everything had to be just right.

I would pick her up at six-ish; we'd drive by the beach where we had first met; we'd arrive at the restaurant where we had our first non-Dutch treat dinner date a year ago; at six-thirty-ish we'd exchange a kiss (maybe two); we'd enter the building.

I would ask for the waiter we had at that first dinner date who would direct us to the very same table. I'd tell her, "Go ahead, my dear, order the steak . . . and lobster." Then the perfect dinner would be followed by coffee. I would be on top, in control, the driver's seat would be mine. All I would have to do would be to turn the key. Yes, the timing would be just right. Low lights, soft music. Everything to make her feel at ease. She would be ready.

Perfect.

Nothing worked right that night. To start with, I never have been all that hot at tying bow ties, but this evening I wasn't even lukewarm. That put me behind ten minutes in picking her up. I hate being late.

And that day, when I was going to wash the car, I had to charge the battery instead . . . it was dead from having left the radio on the night before. So I arrived late in a dirty car. I hate dirty cars, though she didn't seem to mind that much.

I missed the turn-off to the beach and ended up in the backyard garden of someone's summer house. Then she asked me if I was lost. No, I quietly yelled at her, and quickly remembering what must take place that night, I apologized. Why did I have to get upset at a time like that?

Isn't someone on my side? I then leaned over to kiss her but remembered in my haste I had forgotten to brush my teeth so I quickly withdrew. She looked puzzled and asked me if something was wrong. No, I said loudly, wanting to make sure she heard, I was just wondering what nice perfume she was wearing. Of course she didn't believe me.

Inside the restaurant, things went no better. The mood music only made me moodier, "our" waiter had been fired for flirting with female customers and "our" table was taken by an elderly couple, very sterile looking. Our table that evening was by the kitchen.

Some other new discoveries were also made: **95**

cherrystone clams are served live (and I'm not as suave and daring as I had thought) and "beef tripe" is not a fancy name for sirloin but instead a plain name for a cow's stomach lining. I began thinking what hamburger stands would be open late that evening.

O, I groaned. Ohhhh. It'll never work. It'll never happen now. I've really fumbled the ball. Why should I even bother to ask?

I asked. She said yes. I said (to myself), "I don't understand women." She read my mind. She told me that ever since the live cherrystone clams exhibition she knew I was going to ask. Then she told me this:

"I said yes, not because of tonight but because of the last year with you. For all the times you gave me . . . yourself—your time, your love, your overwhelming concern, your desire to see me become a better . . . me. I really doubt if I could have said yes if the past year hadn't been behind us. And I know if I had said no you wouldn't have dropped me and moved on to the next table. You've given me freedom to make up my mind."

"Yes, I will."

Paul Tokunaga is an Inter-Varsity staff member with TWEN-TYONEHUNDRED, the multi-media ministry of IVCF. He graduated from California Polytechnic Institute.

HOME: HOW TO BE SALT TO YOUR FAMILY WITHOUT RUBBING IT IN
JANET CARTER

12

If you ever want to know what it is like to have a sledgehammer held over your head in the name of Jesus, just talk to any member of my family! But if you want to know some of God's mercy, grace and faithfulness in my witness to my once-born family, read on.

Some of our fears of witness and/or compromise as we face the prospect of going home to an unbelieving family for vacation are unfortunately misplaced. And our energies are often misdirected at home as we either argue with or seek to win points by frantic service to our fellow heirs and parent(s). Whether it be fear or fanaticism, neither will be a very effective medium for transmitting the love and grace of the Lord Jesus to our family.

Concerning our family life, we should regard ourselves not as missionaries going to pagan foreign soil, but as ambassadors entering a host country, where courtesy, respect, sensitivity and magnanimity are in order. This is the imagery of Scripture and the reality of our mission. We may face ticklish situations, and in fact we do wage much more than a "cold war" with human ideas, in that our battle is with a host of spiritual forces. However, the One who appoints and sends us is the rightful King and he already reigns in heaven.

losing face and faith "Perfect love casts out fear." If we fear—whether the object be personal compromise, "falling away," persecution or having to explain our position as a Christian—we will not love. Now the question is, Do you want to love your family? Do you experience the love of Christ yourself? Do you desire for them to see him in and through you? God's love can cast away our fears and keep us from falling.

Once upon a time (and in space, of course) God in his great mercy, swallowed all his glory and postponed his rights as King in order to give us his only Son. For a time he willingly gave him to us, sending him to this cold, spiritually barren earth to be an example of perfect love in the face of ridicule and scorn, to endure loneliness and pain, and ultimately to die in the shame of unwarranted criminal execution—all this that we might be healed and restored to God's fellowship with Jesus in his resurrection power.

Does this sound like a cheap God? Like someone

who cannot relate to your fears or your unique

family situation? He knows it all and has ample resources to prepare you and sustain you in your time at home. He even wants to spread his love through you to those around you, as a "fragrance of beauty."

weird wonder "But," you say, "my parents will never understand my position and my brothers and sisters will think I'm positively weird." Well, do *you* think it is weird that you are a Christian? Or are you convinced that you have landed onto Someone pretty wonderful?

I finally said to myself, "Face it, if your parents have cried in concern over you, paid your medical bills, fed and clothed you for all these years, they aren't going to pounce on you *now*, now that you claim to have discovered something that promises to satisfy you completely." I once asked my mother what hopes she had for me, deep down inside, thinking that she probably hoped for me to follow in her profession, or to go to grad school and become a lawyer or something equally amazing. However, she replied thoughtfully that what she wanted most for me was my complete happiness ("though of course I wouldn't mind having grandchildren some day," she added sneakily—mothers are like that).

The catch is, of course, that to really convince your loved ones you are happy, you have to *be* happy. My brother used to complain that all I ever did when I was home from school was read and study. A few months ago as I grabbed brother #1 and teased him into teaching me the latest dance, both brothers were sure I had gone nuts. But they saw a freer, more joyful sister than they ever had during my years of concentrated spirituality.

Most parents do want their children to be deeply satisfied. That does not mean lazy or self-righteous, uncaring or disrespectful. You will most helpfully mirror the love of Jesus to your parents, brothers and sisters as you are grateful to God for the unique family he has given you, being grateful daily for a free gift of salvation in the Lord Jesus Christ, and delighting at every opportunity you can grasp to learn more of life, of people and of our God.

Remember: Assume they love you unless proven otherwise. Parents, just like you and me, have trouble expressing deep feelings. They, too, feel inadequate at times to be totally consistent in their actions.

We are called to honor and obey our parents. Webster defines honor to include "giving credit to" and "giving reverence where it is due." Let's say dad's eyes roam a bit to other women and mom curses and shouts. Does God expect you to respect these qualities and actions? Certainly not. We are not to rejoice in iniquity, but in the truth and in godliness. But it is the Lord's responsibility to deal with the particular sins and shortcomings of your parents, just as with your own. He is the one who knows their hearts, their histories and their circumstances. We are to celebrate *his* life, not legislate theirs. And almost always there are some things in each parent which we can respect.

A critical attitude can powerfully destroy the relationship God has in mind for you and your parents. And no attitudes are picked up more quickly by parent radar than ingratitude and bitterness. They eat away at love and trust, and they hurt parents deeply. We forget all they have done for us, while presuming they will continue to do it. We self-righteously and with complaints compare ourselves to our brothers and sisters. We forget that mom and dad are regular human beings, with personal hopes, tender spots and insecurities. They are not perfect parents and we're not perfect offspring. We must not hold it against them.

that strange habit Or is your fear one of losing touch with God and his Word? This can be disarmed to some extent as you understand the basic issue. You must determine *now* how important your quiet times alone with the Lord are. You may face occasional or repeated pressure to neglect your Bible, or to avoid worship. If your family is offended by a Bible, will you hide it and forget about it, or will you quietly take it to the library to read? How determined are you and how creative will you be? How much in love are you with Christ?

Sometimes we hit periods when our relationship with Jesus is really not all that exciting or productive. Is summertime a secretly welcomed occasion for you to take a vacation from him too? Be honest. If it is, tell him now and ask him to change you. He loves you no matter whether or how much you love him.

Actually, when it comes to family response, your approach to quiet time and Bible reading is much more essential than the actual activity. If your attitude is "devotional" or "spiritual," it will be more resented than if you are simply matter-of-fact about the whole thing. My stepsister came to me one evening recently while I was visiting at home and asked what I was reading. I answered lightly, "the Good Book!" and folded it in my lap temporarily to chat with her. At first she was a bit surprised, and then, because I took it so naturally, she took it naturally. Of course, there were the days not so awfully long ago when I would hole myself up in "my" room to have my quiet time, and even though I put up no signs, PRIVACY PLEASE just oozed out from behind the tightly closed door. My mother would sort of tiptoe around the hall trying to find a place to put my clean, folded clothes but also trying to figure out what in the world made her nunnish daughter tick. Here I was, supposedly loving God and serving people, yet my mom was serving me and I was making it difficult. Your privacy is not sacred, nor do you have a right to expect it in your parents' home. Remember that Jesus had to get up long before day and go out to a lonely place to pray. Ask him for some good ideas—he's been there.

Remember, too, that you are reading a collection of historical writings and Hebrew literature, not to mention four pieces of a unique literary genre: the Gospels. Your parents and family might possibly relate more to this explanation than to the comment that you are reading a Holy Book that is God-breathed, infallible and utterly reliable. You can explain that there is some really great literature in this anthology, and that in presenting what God is like it gives you some very useful teaching on being the person you are intended to be—achieving your potential. Pray that God will guard you from compromise, but remember that (like Jesus and Paul) we speak in different "languages" to different mindsets and understandings.

head bowed, eyes closed Another cloudy area surrounds the questions of conversation and activity in the home. Should you say grace before your meal, even if your family is convinced it just came from the supermarket? What about wine at meals? Theological arguments? Going shopping with your insistent mother to buy piles of new clothes? And on Sunday, no less? Whew! For one thing, the Lord does not expect you to answer them all at once. And again, the attitude with which you join in or decline the activities at hand will make a huge difference in the response of your family.

If you already have a reputation in your family for being pushy or legalistic, I would heartily suggest going easy on the outward expressions of your spirituality. You may have to spend some time convincing your loved ones (by your naturalness) that you really are free in Christ and that Christianity is not just another varied collection of "do's and don'ts." When I was a fairly new Christian, I would insist that we pray before eating (while my two younger brothers squirmed) and then when my uncomfortable mother would resort to always asking *me* to "do it," I would be offended: "Can't anyone else pray?" Well, do I need to tell you that what my family remembers about those days is not my overflowing, grateful attitude which bubbled over in a desire to pray at every opportunity, but my unhappy, restricted self. Again, though, God's mercy is abundant, and now, several years later, I can see my mistake and also his healing. Last Christmas, after I had taken the opportunity to get to know my new stepfather-to-be and shared my Christian perspective on life with him, as well as some doubts and struggles I was having, I was incredulous when he asked me if I would like to say grace at our first Christmas meal together. (I was thankful for a lot **103** more than the gorgeous meal we had at our table that day.)

who can you trust? What about going to non-Christian friends or relatives with personal questions and hassles? What do you share and what do you bear? Perhaps you do not anticipate having much Christian fellowship and support while at home, and think you will have to have at least a three-hour daily quiet time to work through your problems. Well, for one thing, you probably do not have a three-hour quiet time. Second, unless you are transparent about your problems or doubts, they will be revealed in less straightforward ways— you cannot really fool your family. Third, all truth is God's truth, and much wise counsel can be given by people who are "still on the way" spiritually but whose general maturity and experience of life makes them wise. Trust God to help you use their counsel correctly.

During the time shortly after I graduated from high school and before I finally went on to college, I had many personal questions regarding my fatherlessness (my mother was widowed when I was a small child). I was experiencing emotional upheaval upon having to face my future without any inkling whatsoever of what I wanted to do with my life. And I wondered if I really wanted to hassle the whole thing, anyway.

Part of my reluctance to share all this was because I felt my mother was having enough problems of her own raising us three kidlings alone, and perhaps this was justified. But it never occurred to me that some sort of discussion with mom or one of my brothers might aid me in my struggles. I was sure I had to do it all alone, with the help of the Lord, of course, and was afraid that any admission of problems would ruin the chances of their coming to Christ.

Besides the fact that no one comes to repentance by chance, this attitude is really false spirituality. My aloofness cheated my family of two important things during this period: a knowledge of me, their only girl, *and* a clear understanding in their minds that it was not my acclaimed Lord who was having all these hassles; rather, it was me.

it shows I will never forget the day I walked away from my mother after we had had some tense moments talking about all the many Christian activities I was attending. (At the time I was involved in a weekly breakfast Bible study, church three times a week, and a coffeehouse ministry on the weekends. For someone who had once been enmeshed in everything from kite-flying conventions to social work, this was not normal at all.) Mom told me that from what she saw around the house, she knew I could not possibly be happy. I was not, of course, but how dreadful that she could see it. I was offended because it was ridiculous (so I thought) to suppose that a Christian should be unhappy. I was frustrated because my family did not seem to perceive that I had eternal, abundant life—that I had nothing to worry about any more!

You might as well be open about your frustrations and fears around those dear ones who share your towels and toothpaste, because you will never successfully hide them. Pray for greater faith to entrust them to the Lord so you do not have to burden your family (or your Christian family) with your problems; but until you grow in faith and grace, you had better be honest. You may bring some of their deep-seated questions to the surface also and perhaps open the way for them to find answers in the Lord. Being strong does not mean being perfect —it means knowing some of the answers and a lot of the questions, and living on what you have. As we are strong in our security with the Lord, we can relax with our families.

You will miss some of the most fruitful times of friendship and growth with your family if you go home fearing contamination or falling away. What God requires is that we walk humbly with him and seek to do justice among men. He does not appreciate religious overtures and "spiritual" favors. He does not appreciate our worry. What he desires is our full attention, our willingness to keep in close touch with him, to discuss doubtful situations, and to be repentant when he convicts us in our spirits.

If you have a tendency to make your Christian life complicated, your parents, brothers and sisters will be the first to be misled by the smokescreen you put up. If you are honest, they will eventually see the difference God is making in the way you handle life. Relax, and have a good vacation.

Janet Carter has been a program coordinator at Hollygrove, a children's home in Los Angeles. She is a graduate of the University of California at Santa Barbara.

JESUS MADE DISCIPLES
MIKE HAYES

13

As a teacher, Jesus is commonly admired for the clever parables he told. It is often remarked that he chose to convey his teaching in simple, homely little stories, using familiar pastoral elements to make his message more easily grasped by even the most unlearned of people.

Many modern Christians have drawn from this picture of Jesus the lesson that our evangelism ought to so simplify the message of the gospel that anyone who is genuinely seeking truth will be able quickly and easily to accept Jesus Christ as Savior.

Such a view of Jesus and his parables, however, omits two significant facts. First, even for those of us who can reap the benefits of 2,000 years of Bible study, the point of his parables is not at all easy to perceive. Nor was it for the hearers of Jesus' day.

More important, the picture of Jesus using parables to simplify his message directly violates his own teaching on the matter! "To you has been given the secret of the kingdom of God, but for those outside everything is in parables; so that they may indeed see but not perceive, and may indeed hear but not understand; lest they should turn again, and be forgiven" (Mk. 4:11-12).

Jesus' purpose in teaching with parables is quite the opposite of making his message as clear as possible. He seems, rather, to be saying that he wants to make his point deliberately unclear. Even more amazing, his purpose in so doing is to keep people from turning again to be forgiven. Incredible! Can this be the Son of the God who is "not willing that any should perish"?

To ascertain the meaning of this passage we need to examine its immediate setting, Mark 4:1-25. Jesus has just told the parable we now call, somewhat misleadingly, the parable of the sower. His disciples and a few others from the crowd come up to inquire of its meaning. In response to their inquiry Jesus makes his strange remark. He then explains the parable and goes on to add two emphases.

In reading this whole passage, some very basic questions seem to demand immediate attention.

what does the parable mean? In verses 14-40 Jesus explains the parable. It is a warning not to be the kind of person who rejects the Word in the name of popularity; not to be the kind of person who sees the Word only as a source of joy (or, in current terminology, who sees Jesus as simply a wonderful trip); and not to be the kind of person who accepts the validity of the Word but wants to maintain other conflicting values also.

Jesus desires instead that we be those who hear the Word, accept it and bear fruit, thirtyfold, sixtyfold and a hundredfold. The "Word" we may take as the Word of truth or the Word of God or, in this case, the word which Jesus himself was speaking.

What does it mean to "accept" a word? Suppose I tell you, "You will be blinded by this page if you read four more words." You do not believe me! For if you had believed you would not have read on. Likewise, if you believe the Word of God, you will obey it. To believe is to respond appropriately. This is accepting the Word.

Jesus Christ does not wish to aid anyone in an inappropriate response. He does not desire people who commit themselves halfway, who are willing to accept forgiveness without the discipleship to his Word which bears fruit.

why did he speak in parables? His purpose was simply outstanding pedagogy: Do not give an answer until you have helped the learner ask the proper question and find the proper way of seeking answers. How does one find the truth of God? Certainly not simply by hearing a sermon or two—even from Jesus himself—and walking away thinking you have mastered the material.

Jesus came to speak, embody and enact a message of forgiveness. It would have been unfair and unloving to merely talk about it, treating it as nothing more than a concept or an idea. He chose instead a method that forced any honest person to recognize that he or she did not understand. At that point the **109** only honest response was to turn to Jesus and ask for understanding. And that was precisely Jesus' goal!

Why does Jesus speak in parables? So that, as much as possible, no one will hear a significant word until the "soil" has been prepared. And we should learn from his example.

All we are told about the "secret of the kingdom" in a direct way is that it has been given to those who, with the twelve, asked Jesus what he was talking about. Having already explored the answers to our primary questions, however, this fact should not surprise us. For coming to Jesus with an honest, appropriate response to his Word is exactly what Jesus demands of his hearers. The "secret of the kingdom" is nothing more than to hear the Word and act, to hear the Word and respond appropriately.

a way of life What are the lessons we might learn from this passage and from the questions we have asked? For ourselves, the secret of the kingdom is to respond appropriately to the Word of God, even if one can do no more than say, "Jesus, I do not understand," or, "God, I am angry at you," or, "God, I dare not hope anymore." Whatever your honest response to God is at that moment is appropriate and desired by God. It does not matter where you are in your own personal growth. What matters is which way you are moving and growing.

The second lesson concerns evangelism. Evangelism is not a matter of telling a person how easy it is to become a Christian. The task of the Christian is to draw another person out of the unbeliever by

eliciting response. We are not to give answers to

questions that have not been asked. Rather, we are to help people ask the right questions and then give them as much of the Word as they are ready to hear and accept.

To be like Jesus in evangelism, our concern must be to raise questions, to draw out appropriate and honest responses. Surely from Jesus, if not from our own experience in the modern school system, we can learn that simply telling someone something is the world's most ineffective way of communicating significant and life-changing information.

Perhaps now we are ready to take seriously Jesus' repeated insistence that the cost of discipleship is immeasurable. In Luke 14, for example, Jesus warned the people not to think lightly of the prospect of following him: "If any one comes to me and does not hate his own father and mother and wife and children and brothers and sisters, yes, and even his own life, he cannot be my disciple. Whoever does not bear his own cross and come after me, cannot be my disciple" (Lk. 14:26).

In addition to the high cost of being a Christian, two key ideas are suggested by this passage. First, like Jesus and unlike most modern Christians, we must warn a nonbeliever in advance of all that Jesus Christ demands of a Christian. In modern Christendom we have nearly forgotten that Jesus makes demands of us. What little attention we pay to the cost of Christianity is normally shared only with those who have already stepped through the door of salvation. Our unwritten policy seems to be to sell them the product before we tell them the price. This is deceitful evangelism.

The second concept is closely related to the first, although more basic. Jesus' words—as well as the whole of the New Testament—lay a great stress upon becoming *disciples*, not mere converts. Of all the biblical ideas which have been lost or compromised over the centuries, this is the most significant. God's goal is to gain obedient disciples of Jesus Christ, not merely to have a population explosion in heaven! Time and time again, Jesus calls followers, stresses obedience, warns that his way demands all or nothing.

In modern evangelical circles we stress that the way to become a Christian is to "accept Jesus as personal Savior." The call of the Bible, however, is to accept Jesus as Lord if you desire to be saved, and then he will be your Savior. We should not accept him just to avoid hell, for becoming a Christian is not a matter of receiving infallible life insurance. It is a matter of giving to God in Christ that which he deserves.

As we might expect, Jesus not only exemplified proper evangelism but also taught us a great deal about it. On his last evening with the disciples before his crucifixion, for example, evangelism was very much on his mind: "By this all men will know that you are my disciples"—note that he did not say converts—"if you have love for one another" (Jn. 13:35). Later in the evening, he prayed in a similar vein "that they may all be one; even as thou, Father, art in me, and I in thee, that they also may be in us, so that the world may believe that thou hast sent me" (Jn. 17:21).

On this final evening, Jesus was thinking of evangelism as the Christians' mutual love and fellowship in God the Father and in himself as Son.

How unlike modern evangelism! Today evangelism is thought of as the pattern of words we speak when we are trying to persuade someone to become a Christian. Evangelism has become, like all else in our secular society, a technique, a way of doing things.

Rather than being an activity in which we may occasionally choose to participate, evangelism is a way of life. It is a life lived continually in discipleship.

Mike Hayes has been a staff member for Inter-Varsity in Honolulu for several years.

THE LAST STEP IS THE FIRST
WILLIAM YORK

14

A new baby is more than a statistic. Not many parents set the newborn on the back step of the hospital and then leave by the front door exclaiming how nice it is to have another child. Birth is the beginning of a long growing process in which the child needs lots of help. The baby needs to be with people, needs feeding and eventually needs to be taught how to take care of himself. Then he or she will be able to care for children of his or her own.

With spiritual rebirth it is the same. If you are privileged to help another person enter into new life in Christ, your responsibility does not end there. Do not leave the new Christian on a doorstep and rejoice about your statistic. You must help the person to grow. If a newborn child of God arrives in your neighborhood and you find out he is there, don't just say, "Isn't that nice, that makes four of us." Feed him. People can die from spiritual malnutrition. Here are some suggestions for helping a new Christian.

assurance Immediately after a person has invited Jesus Christ into his life, give a scriptural basis for assurance that Christ has indeed come in. Encourage him or her to read the Bible regularly.

Do not give a person *your* assurance that he is now a Christian. The only true and adequate assurance must come from the witness of the Holy Spirit within that person (Rom. 8:15-16). Show the spiritual babe verses from God's Word which the Holy Spirit can use to give true assurance.

You might say something like the following:

"There is a verse in Scripture which describes the step you have just taken. [Turn to Revelation 3:20 and read it.] Jesus Christ is knocking at the door of people's lives. When they open the door, he goes in to live with them. We have his Word for that, and we accept it by faith. When people have Jesus Christ they *have* eternal life. [Turn to 1 John 5:11-12 and read it.]

"You will find that learning from Jesus Christ and obeying him as your Lord will not always be easy, but it will be challenging and satisfying. His primary means of teaching you will be the Bible. [Turn to 2 Timothy 3:16-17 and read it.] What we learn from the Bible is 'food' which helps us grow in our new life, and we need to read it regularly just as we need to eat regularly.

"In order to get the most out of the Bible, it is **115**

helpful to have a guide to study by. Here is a little study guide that has readings for each day for a month. [Give him or her *First Mornings with God.*] It takes about twenty minutes per reading. I suggest that you pick a time each day to go through one. You might make it the first thing you do after you get dressed in the morning, so you will be starting every day with instruction from the Lord.

"How about our getting together again day after tomorrow to talk over some of the things you learn from your Bible reading?"

Check to be sure your friend has a Bible. If he does not, lend him one, preferably a modern translation, until you can go to a bookstore with him and help him pick a good Bible with decent-sized print. If he has a Bible, but it is a King James Version (seventeenth-century English) in small print and you feel that a modern version would be more comprehensible, suggest the Revised Standard Version, Berkeley Version or New English Bible.

the next appointment By now, following *First Mornings with God,* he or she will have read John 3:1-21 and John 4:1-26. If so, discuss the "new birth." (Have a copy of *First Mornings with God* with you. If not, read the two passages, go through the first day's reading together and proceed as follows. Encourage the newborn to begin the readings with "Day 2" the next morning.)

Ask what was learned about how the new birth occurs. Your friend may not have thought he was "born again" when he received Jesus Christ, so discuss the fact that when people receive Christ, they are born into a new life.

116 Talk over privileges of the new life, which include prayer and guidance from God in decisions we face. God is willing to help us in every aspect of our lives, including how we spend our money and our free time. You can consider together these things in prayer.

Discuss problems of the new life. Introduce the fact that we have an enemy, Satan, who will try to keep us from learning from the Lord and growing spiritually. Satan will tempt us to sin and will try to keep us living a self-centered life rather than giving ourselves wholeheartedly to the Lord. But the Lord lives in us and is stronger than Satan. As we ask him for help we can overcome the problems. Talk about what to do when we sin. Show him from 1 John 1:9 that we must confess sin to the Lord and he will forgive us.

You could suggest a reading course that is designed to help people grow spiritually. The one I recommend here consists of three Bible study guides (one of which you have already given) and seven small books to read in sequence. The first one to give is *Being a Christian* by John Stott. Ask him to read it before you meet again, when you will give the second one. (Explain that you are following a definite reading outline of seven books. This may make the person more apt to read the books than if you simply begin feeding a steady stream of books.)

Pray together. Encourage a few sentences of verbal prayer. Keep your own prayer brief and simple. Also encourage continual Bible reading and make an appointment for two days later.

the second follow-through appointment

By now he or she will have read John 4:27-42, and the comments on witnessing in *First Mornings with* **117**

God and *Being a Christian*. (Be sure you are familiar with both.)

Discuss the privilege Christians have of telling others about how they can have new life by receiving Jesus Christ. Talk over how the Lord can help him to live a life that will attract the interest of friends and acquaintances (giving a new love for people, a new spirit of helpfulness, a new joy and so on). Pray together that the Lord will help you both live in ways that will open opportunities to talk about Jesus Christ.

If there are other Christians with whom you are meeting for prayer, let this new Christian know that you find it helpful and encouraging. Invite him to attend the next prayer meeting with you.

Give him Robert Munger's booklet *My Heart–Christ's Home*. Explain that it is a good booklet on how Christ can help with every part of life, and ask that it be read before your next appointment. Make that appointment for about three days later.

literature for continued follow-through At the third follow-through appointment lend him or her *The Fight* by John White. Explain that it is a good, practical handbook on living the Christian life. Suggest that he read a chapter a day, and let you know when it is finished, so you can give the next book in the series.

After reading *The Fight*, lend *Quiet Time*. It has helpful suggestions for a daily time of Bible reading and prayer. Suggest reading it within a day or two.

After reading *Quiet Time*, lend him *Basic Christianity* by John Stott, explaining that it is an excellent introduction to the person and work of Christ. Suggest reading it within two weeks.

Next, lend Stott's *Basic Introduction to the New Testament.* It is a very good, brief introduction to the writings of the New Testament. Suggest reading it within three weeks.

The last book in the series is *Knowing God* by J. I. Packer. Lend it, explaining that it is an overall introduction to the major doctrines of God. This one may also take about three weeks to read.

After the first month the Bible study guide *First Mornings with God* should have been completed. You could replace it with *Christ in You,* a personal study guide that should not take more than two weeks to go through during daily Bible reading.

After completing *Christ in You,* offer *This Morning with God, Volume I* or *Grow Your Christian Life.*

Continue to meet with your new Christian friend at least once a week. If you do not have a planned appointment, at least meet for a meal or other informal activity. Be a friend. Read the Bible together and encourage him to continue his own Bible reading. Pray together—this will be the best training in prayer. Share some of your own prayer requests and problems. He will get discouraged if he thinks you have no problems and he has many. Just be honest—do not try to act like something you are not.

Pray daily. It is still the work of the Holy Spirit to teach and cause him or her to grow.

Be a good listener, so he will share his joys and problems with you.

Discuss the best way to tell friends and family that a change has taken place. It is best to be open and honest about the changes, not artificial. It is also very important that the new Christian not antagonize others when he or she first discusses the topic **119** with friends and family.

Introduce him to other Christians in a Bible study, a prayer group or a church. But don't be pushy. You are asking him or her to add more activities to what may already be a full schedule. At first he may have no awareness of the need for Christian fellowship and Bible teaching. You may have to work it in slowly. It would be easy to overwhelm your friend with invitations to a number of time-consuming activities.

exceptions to the rule Sometimes new Christians will start out in the Christian life like a rocket. The Bible is so interesting and exciting that they cannot read it enough. Instead of going through *First Mornings with God* a day at a time, they will read the entire Gospel of John in the first two days. Be ready to suggest what to read next. After John's Gospel, recommend Acts (a history of the development of the early church), then Ephesians (a letter to a young church with good advice for young Christians), then another of the Gospels and on into Paul's letters.

The series of seven books you are giving will have some suggestions on Bible study which will help. Occasionally a new Christian will spend so much time in Bible study and other Christian reading and activities that his other obligations (family, work, school) will begin to suffer. If this seems to be the case, counsel him on the need to fulfill his duties to honor Christ. Emphasize the need for discipline and recommend a systematic daily study of the Bible and Christian books for a set period of time.

At the other extreme, some who have just invited Christ into their lives may not respond at all to your suggestions for Bible study and other reading. These people must be worked with patiently until a spiritual appetite develops.

Just as we do not expect a new mother to hand her baby a cookbook when he is two weeks old and say, "I'll be back tonight. Make yourself a nice lunch. There's lots of stuff in the refrigerator," so we cannot expect a brand new believer to survive without help from the family into which he has been born. When you commit yourself to doing evangelism, remember that means follow-through too.

William York has served on Inter-Varsity staff in Virginia. He is also the author of One to One, *an evangelistic Bible study guide.*

PART 5
CAMPUS
STRATEGY

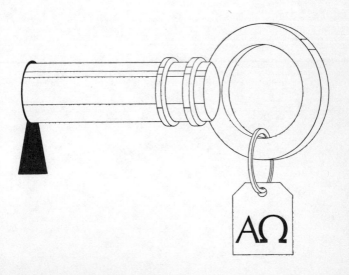

SPYING OUT THE LAND

ANDREW T. LE PEAU

15

God has a vision of what he wants for the whole of his creation. "For he has made known to us in all wisdom and insight the mystery of his will, according to his purpose which he set forth in Christ as a plan for the fulness of time, to unite all things in him, things in heaven and things on earth" (Eph. 1: 9, 10). He has a plan for your campus too.

In the fall, however, a group of Christian students too often finds its activities planned as a haphazard list: Bible studies, prayer meetings, hayrides, booktables and so on and so on. No sense of priorities. No sense of proportion. No time or work spent on making things fit. And why this particular list? "It's what we did last year," or "It worked at another school nearby." But each Inter-Varsity chapter is unique, and even more important, each *campus* is unique. Dartmouth is different from Arizona State is different from the University of Saskatchewan. God's plan ("to unite all things in him") gets "fleshed out" on a campus in accord with the unique characteristics of that campus. You cannot expect the same activities to be equally effective on very dissimilar campuses.

ask for a vision To develop a vision that is unique to your campus, you need to begin with prayer. God is our guide and has promised to be with us even to the end of the age. Pray that he will instill in you a desire for penetrating the major areas of your campus—geographically, academically and socially. Do you believe this is God's will for your chapter? Do you then believe God is able to accomplish it through you? If so, you can pray in confidence.

Pray, too, that he will guide you and your fellow chapter leaders as you discuss how you will carry out this vision. As I said, each campus is different. So your discussion should begin by finding out what your campus is like. Ask, How many students are there and in what categories (grads, undergrads, majors)? Where are they located (dorms, frats, apartments)? What significant minorities are there? How many students have jobs?

Also ask, What is the mood or atmosphere (cold, friendly, apathetic)? What exerts an influence on students (Black Muslims, Kurt Vonnegut, the school newspaper)? How have things changed in the last few years (declining enrollment, more faculty unrest, less social life)? What religious organizations are on campus, how big are they and what influence do they have?

Questions like these (and others you may think of) can help you to spy out the land God has given you to conquer. Numbers 13 tells how Moses evaluated Canaan: He had twelve spies spend forty days just observing it. Obviously this was no small task. But without it the people would have had no basis for a wise decision about what they should do.

You must begin by observing (even though it may involve a dry collecting of facts) before you can evaluate the difficulties and opportunities which face you.

develop a strategy After getting a solid foundation, you need correct analysis and planning. Most of Moses' spies gave an incorrect evaluation. It cost Israel a generation. So let us say you answer these questions and find out that on your campus of 10,000, half are grad students who are mostly commuters, the undergrads live mostly in dorms, and academic standards are quite high in a very competitive and socially cold atmosphere. What might be the strategy to penetrate your campus?

Grads and undergrads usually have strikingly different needs. This is heightened on your campus because the two groups have very different living situations. Perhaps your ideal chapter would be two chapters with two distinct programs, each meeting the particular needs of one of the primary groups. Yet both chapters would probably emphasize (1) an intellectual foundation for the Christian faith in the face of harsh skepticism and (2) strong friendships in a loving community to overcome, and stand out in contrast to, the campus's coldness.

Or let us say you answer the above questions and discover that on your campus of 17,000, most are undergrads who live on campus, football is the only thing that excites the whole school and social activities take up the bulk of free time in a friendly and congenial setting. How might you penetrate the campus?

Focusing on the dorms is one way. You could also take advantage of the football mania and gain visibility by sponsoring buses to a nearby away game for the campus. And while there would be other ways of plugging into the campus social scene, the chapter could exhibit deep commitment to Christ and to fellow Christians and so stand out in stark contrast on a campus which majors in superficial relationships and has little dedication to values.

These are only two examples of how you could develop a campuswide vision by taking advantage of (1) the peculiar, unique characteristics of your campus in general and (2) the peculiar needs that your chapter can speak to, in effectively presenting the gospel. Let your imagination have full play when you do this for your school. Do not limit yourself. Assume, for the moment, that you have all the resources of time, people and money that you need. The key is to mold the chapter to the campus and so create the ideal "fellowship for evangelism" unit for *your* campus. Do not fool yourself into thinking you can make the campus fit your fellowship.

This does not mean that you adopt the values or purposes of your campus, but that you, like Paul, "become all things to all men, that [you] might by all means save some" (1 Cor. 9:22). You identify with your campus. But you also confront it at its point of need, not ignoring its inadequacies.

return to reality Yet after finding ourselves in the rarefied air of unbounded imagination, we must, nonetheless, return to terra firma. "Have two separate chapters? We barely have one, and only three or four grad students are involved!" Okay— if you are to aim at the ideal chapter, you must know where your starting point is.

Go back and look at the questions you asked about your campus. Now ask them about your chapter. And in addition ask such questions as, What activities did the fellowship attempt last year and with what amount of success? How many are in the core and how many in the fringe? Has the group been reaching out or reaching in? Why? What structure does the fellowship have (network of small groups, the exec does all the work, or another)?

If you have three or four grad students, start with a grad Bible study. It will probably take three or four years to develop a good-sized group. Plan on that. In fact, let the grad students do the planning.

If ninety per cent of your chapter is off campus and ninety per cent of the campus lives in the dorms, things need to change. Start with small steps like a few people volunteering to move back into the dorms. But realize that a long-range plan will be necessary to bring things into the balance you want. Work up some goals for where you want the chapter to be one, two and three years from now with concrete suggestions for getting there.

In summary begin by praying that God will give you his vision for reaching your whole campus— for what "conquer the land" will mean there. Then spy out the land he has given you. Observe your chapter as well. Next, evaluate both, looking for key characteristics and needs you can use to your advantage. Then apply your findings by making broad goals. Imagine what the ideal chapter would be like for your unique campus, then mold your present resources and program to the campus. Finally, make some specific suggestions for bringing your chapter from where it is now to where your vision says it should be in two, three or four years.

God has a vision for your campus. Open your eyes to see your campus and you will see God's vision too.

Andrew T. Le Peau is an assistant editor with InterVarsity Press. He served on Inter-Varsity staff in St. Louis for two years.

TRANSLATING THE GOSPEL INTO GREEK

EDWARD FOCHT

16

Sometimes we disregard people and places in our outreach for God. Subtle stereotypes infiltrate our thinking, blinding us to real needs of others and taking away opportunities in which God can use us.

Have you prayerfully considered outreach to fraternities and sororities on your campus? Or have you simply disregarded that possibility? Have you spied out the promised land crossing the Jordan at God's command? Have you visited the houses to meet the "beer-drinking, fun-loving, materialistically motivated, sex-starved" collegiates, who in reality are not that much different from you?

They doubt, fear and hurt just as you do. The difference is you find solace and peace in the Lord

Jesus Christ, while they may find solace in other people, owning things, smoking pot or drinking.

I grant there are dangers in becoming deeply involved with non-Christians, especially if you infiltrate a Greek house to share the claims of Christ by word and example. But if you are truly under Jesus Christ's lordship and motivated to serve him, guided by God's Holy Spirit, he will take those dangerous situations and develop them into stretching experiences that eventually will glorify himself.

Perhaps you have not seriously considered going Greek because doing so seemed unscriptural. One principle forbids mismatch with unbelievers (2 Cor. 6:14). When Christians overlook this principle for marriage, untold problems and heartaches result. But marriage lasts a lifetime, whereas active fraternity or sorority involvement lasts four years or less. Your level of commitment is set in marriage, but it is flexible in a Greek house. Because of this the principle of becoming as a Jew in order to win the Jews (1 Cor. 9:9-23) takes precedence. We are called to be separated from sin, not isolated from the sinner. We are to be transformed into the image of Jesus Christ, not to be conformed to this world. Jesus stated unequivocally that we are the salt of the earth (Mt. 5:13). How are we to provide flavoring if we remain in the salt shaker? As salt dissolves on meat, it loses its crystalline structure as its flavor permeates the meat. Christians should slip out of their isolating containers and provide flavoring where it is needed.

sacrifice Joining a fraternity or sorority means personal sacrifice, sacrifice which hurts. One sacrifice I experienced was making myself vulnerable to the other fraternity brothers in terms of ridicule and frustration. The ridicule which came from nonbelievers the first year slowly ceased as I prayed and walked consistently. The frustration resulted from a relationship with a professed Christian in the house who was not as willing as I was to make the time commitments and character changes necessary to see the kingdom of God develop in the fraternity. This experience taught me to walk according to Jesus' example and standards, not my brothers'. God dealt with my bitterness as I spoke to the Lord about it. I am thankful for the experience because I got to know God better through it.

Very possibly a sacrifice will include not developing a deep involvement with a person of the opposite sex in order to spend quality time with the brothers. Making friendships in the house must be one of your top priorities. Of course, living in the same house with other people does not guarantee quality relationships.

Another sacrifice I made so that I could spend time with the brothers was settling for a 2.78 average instead of striving for a higher one. Your grades do not automatically fall if you join the Greeks, but I found I had to study less than I desired so that I could be a brother in more than just name.

Saying good-by to my privacy was another sacrifice. Not only in terms of sleep, but also in time that I could call my own. Often discussions or counseling sessions would arise late at night which warranted my presence when I would have preferred to sleep. I maintained an open-door policy so anyone could enter whenever he wished. As a result, I could not study well in my room. I made it a policy to go to the library whenever I had to get something **133** done. I could have remained more isolated, but that would have deterred the openness vital for seeing God's kingdom grow.

As I sacrificed, God showed me principles dealing with guilt, guidance and priorities. Because I only hoped God would use me, instead of being sure that God had called me into the fraternity, I was susceptible to an undercurrent of doubt. This doubt enabled Satan to manipulate my thinking as he haunted me with a nebulous guilt feeling. He kept me timid and almost ineffective in outreach my first six months in the house. I realized during a weekend training conference that I had not been serving God with a clear conscience as Paul had (2 Tim. 1:3). I shared this nebulous guilt feeling with a girl, who said that it had to be caused by Satan, because God is specific concerning guilt. Since I knew of no unconfessed sin in my life, I agreed with her and rebuked Satan's manipulatory powers over me. The guilt subsided and I became more bold in outreach. I invited a team from Campus Crusade for Christ to give their testimonies after dinner one night. As a result, two brothers made decisions for Christ. Even though they fell away during the summer, the ice had been broken.

harvest time The next year, my last, was spent cultivating the field with Bible studies, times of prayer and fasting, and one-on-one conversations as other Christians were led to join the fraternity. The harvest came when the brothers allowed me to give a challenging speech centering on accepting Jesus as Savior and Lord during one of our last major functions of the year. Fifteen out of forty brothers stood to either commit or recommit their lives to Christ. Seeing them stand took the sting out of the previous frustration. The guilt that I had experienced was now simply a part of the past.

Another principle I learned was that I could never spend as much time as I desired with the brothers and still be effectively used by him. He was constantly giving me opportunities for training and learning which had to take priority over my fraternity involvement. This feeling of constantly being torn from the brothers to engage in Bible studies, prayer watches, fellowship meetings and weekend conferences forced me to depend upon God to work when I was not there. He did work. As a result, respect for me and for his message increased even though the time that I could spend with the brothers didn't. But the increased respect did not lessen the hurt I felt when I was torn from good involvement with them for better involvement with God.

No matter where you are located as a Christian, whether in your family, school, business or dating involvements, your character growth and effectiveness in spreading God's kingdom increase only as your own personal sacrifices increase. This is cold fact. Jesus said, "If any man would come after me, let him deny himself and take up his cross daily and follow me" (Lk. 9:23). The scalpel of sacrifice slices away all the extras of the world, so that we can enjoy the really abundant life with him.

A third principle related to the sacrifice of being torn from the brothers is that of praying for them. I almost let my activities as president of the Inter-Varsity chapter justify my lack of intercession for both Christians and non-Christians. As I did a character study on Moses throughout my senior year, **135**

God started to impress upon me the importance of concentrated prayer and fasting. Twice Moses, while he was responsible for over a million Israelites, extricated himself from his busy routine to be with God for forty straight days and nights. I found myself hard pressed to set aside one hour a week on Sunday to pray for my associates. As I hesitantly gave up more time to him in prayer and fasting, he worked first in me and then spoke to others.

As my intercession for individuals became more specific, he worked in my heart to melt away my pride and fill it with a greater love for them. I became more aware of them as people who hurt. I learned to empathize with their problems instead of judging them because of their sins. The final result was increased communication, openness and growth in God's kingdom. My only regret about fraternity involvement is that I did not grasp these principles sooner. Had that happened, the fraternity could very well have changed by now to be based not simply on a social brotherhood but on the rock of Christ.

guidance How can you know whether God is leading you into a fraternity or sorority where you would grow not only in character but also as a useful channel of God? First are you growing in your relationship with Christ? Do you desire to read God's Word, to talk with him, and to apply what he shows you to your personal life? Is he transforming you into the likeness of his Son as a potter would mold a piece of clay into a useful vessel?

Are you turning your problems over to God? The general principle is to center our thoughts on God and his Word, rather than on ourselves and our problems. For example, one potential problem area is sexual temptation. Do you fantasize about sexual activity or do you at the point of temptation "turn it over to God"? To turn temptation over to God, first tell God that you are aware of the temptation, and if you have sinned, ask him for forgiveness. Thank him on the spot for forgiving you, and then replace the thought with a verse or two from a meaningful hymn, a mental picture of Jesus Christ or Scripture such as "How can a young man keep his way pure? By guarding it according to thy word. I have laid up thy word in my heart, that I might not sin against thee" (Ps. 119:9, 11). If you have God's Word stored up in your heart, and claim the promise in 1 Corinthians 10:13, that you will not be tempted beyond your strength, you will successfully combat temptation. Yielding control to God in specific areas of your life is the basic requirement for fraternity involvement.

Second, is God guiding you to at least one other Christian willing to join the house? Jesus sent the disciples out two by two, so when one fell or became discouraged, the other was available for support and encouragement, both in word and in prayer. The fraternity is no exception. But both of you must be totally committed to presenting each other mature in Christ through gut-level character change.

One last word about the pressure of Greek Rush. Do not be swayed by the glib tongue of a Greek to join prematurely. You should establish relationships with members of at least three houses before you pledge. Tactfully share your beliefs and motivation for joining as God leads. If you are a freshman, pledge during your sophomore year. If you are a sophomore, wait until spring. You will be pressured to be quantity-time oriented instead of quality-time oriented from the start. Stand your ground and do not let your priorities become confused. Remember, getting to know God is first, studies come second, and Greek involvement is third.

Sacrifice, cost, vulnerability, frustration, discouragement, hope and being involved in the growth of the kingdom: Will you allow yourself to be jarred from the shaker and dissolved so Jesus Christ's flavor spreads?

Edward Focht was active in local chapters of Theta Chi fraternity and Inter-Varsity Christian Fellowship while at the U. of Cincinnati. He is currently a construction supervisor looking, with his wife, toward missionary service in Pakistan.

GROUP WITNESS
DON SMITH

17

Are you bothered because you have found evangelism awkward? Consider an important slant on the subject of Christian witness as the Bible presents it: Apart from someone who has a special gift of evangelism, the most effective display of Jesus Christ to the world comes through a group of Spirit-filled Christians acting together, not through a Christian operating independently.

The biblical logic which supports this is quite simple. Paul identifies the whole church (meaning all born-again believers rather than an institution) as the body of Christ: "You are the body of Christ and individually members of it" (1 Cor. 12:27). Any one Christian may be an eye or a corpuscle or a joint or a big toe, but the church—a group of people—is the body of Christ. If the world is to see Christ, attention should not be directed primarily to one member of the body, but to a group of Christians who are expressing more of Christ's gifts and who are being knit together in his love. A non-Christian sees more of Jesus Christ if he sees more of his people.

A biblical model for such a witnessing community is the Jerusalem church described in Acts 2:42-47. These Christians were "praising God and having favor with all the people. And the Lord added to their number day by day those who were being saved" (v. 47). Their community was a visible expression of Christ to the unbelievers around them. God used their corporate witness as well as the witness of men with special gifts in evangelism, men like the Apostle Peter.

If this hypothesis about group witness is correct, it has at least two important corollaries. The first is that I do not need to be a carbon copy of any other Christian. God wants me to function as a unique part of the body, not to try to fill someone else's role. Paul recognizes the temptation to be dissatisfied with one's own role when he writes, "If the ear should say, 'because I am not an eye, I do not belong to the body,' that would not make it any less a part of the body. If the whole body were an eye, where would be the hearing? . . . As it is, there are many parts, yet one body" (1 Cor. 12:16-17, 20). Another image which illustrates this is an army. In a battle every soldier does not handle the same weapon or attack from the same position. Similarly, God wants each of us to fulfill the unique place he has for us, rather than to try to stand in another's place.

The second corollary is that I am not obliged to reveal all of Christ to every non-Christian. I am not the entire body. My personality cannot offer the most appropriate witnessing style to attract the interest of every non-Christian. Some will respond to my individual expression of Christ in the world; others will be unimpressed. But if any non-Christian sees me operating in a Spirit-filled group of Christians he should be able to recognize that Jesus' life transcends any one personality-type or lifestyle. This does not imply that God does not require or use individual witness. However, a Christian should realize that his own witness can be, and perhaps should be, augmented by that of a community.

This approach supports the action group concept which is important in Inter-Varsity's campus strategy. The small group, seen and heard by those who do not know Christ, can be a vital witness within a university. Activities like a pizza party can be planned in order to introduce non-Christians to the body of Christ. The group supports and magnifies the witness of each individual member.

Can this evangelistic theory be realized today? Some of my recent experiences indicate it can. I have talked with two people who have been converted within the last year because of the influence of a small group of Christians. One met the Lord through a Bible study, and the other, through a prayer group. The first person explained that a friend had invited him to a Bible study at which he saw "such love in everyone's face and was so aware of the presence of Jesus" that he gave his life to Christ. The other said she was excited by the joy and honest sharing among the members of the prayer group. Both people now have a solid relationship with Christ and seem to have grown significantly in a short time as Christians.

I also have seen some people converted because of the witness of a larger community. In my city a weekly Catholic-Protestant prayer meeting which attracts several hundred people is having an exciting evangelistic impact. A fellow with whom I discussed Christianity last year committed his life to Christ this summer because of his encounter with that group. I have also been able to observe that a Christian summer camp community not only has an effect on Christians who attend, but also makes a strong evangelistic appeal to unbelievers who come into contact with it.

This may stimulate your campus fellowship to concentrate more on a group presentation of Christ. Then each Christian can be free to find his unique place in God's plan for the world.

Don Smith was an Inter-Varsity staff member in Michigan for several years. Presently he is adult curriculum editor with David C. Cook Publishing Co.

A CASE STUDY IN CAMPUS EVANGELISM: MIAMI U. OF OHIO

C. STEPHEN BOARD

18

OXFORD, OHIO: Inter-Varsity at Miami University is a helpful illustration of how a group can lay a solid foundation and then build an intensive campus witness on that foundation. Evangelism is going on at Miami, but it is evangelism in the context of much more. There are some principles being practiced by the group on this campus that can be used on any campus in the country.

Miami U. is a state university with some 13,000 students in residence; it is co-ed and moderately selective. The students are not flaming radicals, but you do not see any going to class in suits either. The humanities dominate the ethos of the place. The campus bookstore, that ineluctable gauge of what goes at a college, has a window filled with such paperbacks as Kubrick's *A Clockwork Orange*, Camus's *The Rebel*, Rollo May's *Man in Search of Himself* and Thoreau's *Walden* writings. Most of the students live on the campus with its consistent Georgian architecture so unlike the crazy quilt mixture of hotels and classical temples that usually afflicts state universities. So much for the externals.

Standing amid the robust secularism of Miami are several Christian groups. Inter-Varsity has been here for a couple of decades, and the Miami chapter is presently one of the most vigorous chapters in the country. About one hundred twenty students show up at the biweekly chapter meetings, and more than that are involved in the dormitory fellowship groups that make up the expanding edge of IVCF on this campus. Campus Crusade has begun in the last few years at Miami, and a fairly good working relationship between these two groups has developed, aided by the fact that many I-V kids and Crusaders attend the same church. Some denominational organizations like Chi Alpha (Assemblies of God), the Baptist Student Union (Southern Baptists) and the Campus Christian Fellowship (Christian Church) exercise a conserving influence on their own young people and, to some extent, confront the multitudes.

Before examining the nature of the Inter-Varsity chapter I must mention the mood that comes across as you visit the regular Christians on this campus. The people in the chapter know they are led by a team of more mature Christians who are dead serious about having an impact for God at Miami. The exec, the dormitory team leaders and the IVCF staff man, Barney Ford, and his wife impress you as people of conviction and discipline. This no-nonsense leadership filters down through the ranks with an effect that no chapter structure, evangelism gimmicks or other short cuts could possibly achieve.

A junior sociology major who is vigorous in witness for Christ says: "It has a lot to do with Barney. He just lays it down and you know it's true and you have to do it. At first I had trouble being comfortable around him; I fought the discipline idea—it seemed so structured in comparison to the fellowship I had at home." Barney, who has been the Inter-Varsity representative at Miami for three years, is not known for dwelling on his uncertainties. I was not surprised to find his influence on many of the students on campus. Nor was I surprised to learn that one of his favorite movies was *Patton*.

The chapter has been building in the basics for several years. "One of the reasons we have been able to grow is that the body of Christ has been healthy in foundational truths—the place of prayer, a disciplined quiet time and faith that God is at work," Barney told me. This pays off in evangelism. When someone becomes a Christian he knows what it will mean because he's had Christians around to observe. Two and a half years ago sixty students became Christians, and fifty-eight of them are known to be still moving in the Christian life. They knew what they were getting into and paid the price.

The chapter president, Doug Calhoun, became a Christian his sophomore year after a fraternity evangelistic presentation—the first time he had heard the gospel. About ten male students became believers at that time in answer to the chapter's prayer for more men in their group. Immediately after becoming a Christian, Doug was given a fraternity brother who asked him dozens of difficult questions about Christianity and who later came to faith. This early stimulation to learn and the experience of getting help from God prepared Doug for the leadership he now offers. He shared with me some of the Miami chapter's policies.

chapter structure The chapter has a distinctive structure and a set of distinctive goals. It has an executive committee with the standard offices and then has the campus divided into quads. This geographical division is credited with much of the effectiveness of their evangelistic outreach. Formerly, all fellowship groups were randomly thrown together, depending on schedule and other arbitrary factors. Now each dorm has a team of Christians responsible for the evangelization of their dorm. The team is led by a team leader. The team leader is in touch with a quad coordinator, who is a communications link between the exec and the dorm teams.

One person reported, "We've been pushed to a stronger idea of authority. We now tell people, 'God has put you there to do a job and to represent him. If he's put you there he'll give you the resources to do it. You don't have to wait until you go to an IVCF camp or until you are older in Christ.' " A junior, Alison Hurt, who became a Christian through Young Life before college, told me: "From the beginning God put it in my heart to be in the sorority for him. Even when I was a freshman and didn't know much about the lordship of Christ, a girl came to me and saw I was 'into religion,' as she put it, and suggested we start a group. So we prayed about it and started a Bible study that has been going for two years now, and many have come to Christ through it."

The exec makes no decisions for a particular dorm. Each dorm team plots its own strategy in cooperation with the exec. If the exec detects that a ball is being dropped in a particular dorm, they approach the quad coordinator who then approaches the dorm team leader. This format keeps the chapter structure virtually invisible to the average person. The leadership serves the teams; the teams are forced to grow on their own and trust God for help. The real action is taking place in the living units where it is visible to the nonbelievers.

How do the campuswide I-V meetings fit into this format? They are teaching sessions that include fellowship and praise. Speakers are invited to address areas defined by the chapter's written goals, which were prepared before the year began. (Note that the speaker is not invited merely to "say what's on his heart," a haphazard use of a large group meeting.) When David Adeney spoke to the whole chapter, it was to advance the chapter's specific goal of heightening their consciousness of world missions.

spreading the word When it comes to evangelism, the chapter likewise works toward specific goals, even while leaving implementation to the geographical teams. One goal is to "increase our understanding of evangelism as a way of life." This leads to an emphasis on friendship evangelism and training in the evangelistic message. Dianne, who has been a Christian a couple of months, shared **147**

with me: "It was the biggest soft sell of the century for me. I would never have responded to a hard-sell approach." She reviewed an experience two years before: "Alison sat down at the dinner table and just happened to say, 'I became a Christian five years ago.' I decided I had to get to know her, and I found I was bumping into her all the time. I was astounded. The minute I started seriously looking for Christ, Christians were coming out of the woodwork. And I could see these were real people.

Contact evangelism—confrontation with total strangers—is used at Miami as a training experience, but not as the primary means of outreach. A leader from last year's exec, Dave Gill, says: "Contact evangelism is a way of getting people to be free in friendship evangelism. As you have more experience sharing the content of the gospel you can be more relaxed to concentrate on the individual person. Your boldness grows from contact evangelism." This is why training of younger Christians at Miami often involves pairing up to do contact work in the student union or other campus meeting places. They also use one-to-one training in the dorms doing contact work with the existing acquaintances of the younger Christians. This combines the advantages of both methods, training the Christian and supplementing an existing friendship.

"These kids know how to share, get the facts across and then ask for a decision," Barney says. "Asking for a decision keeps friendship evangelism from being more friendship than evangelism."

"Often in friendships we want to make people feel comfortable so we let our conversation slip away," Alison told me. "We've learned to find where people are and show them where the line is and what they have to do. I had a problem just being afraid of some girls—they seemed happy, good-looking and had lots of dates. But now I'm convinced that everyone, without exception, is looking for something. So many kids are searching now; it's phenomenal. Day and night there are people coming around asking questions."

This may explain why Dianne, the new Christian mentioned above, says, "I could see people living their faith. This brought me to Christ and helped me most afterward. They let the Holy Spirit work through them. My biggest question was, What difference will it make? They were the answer."

boldness and training Two themes keep emerging at Miami: the emphasis on boldness and the emphasis on training by example. One student told me, "Last year Barney had some teaching sessions and he stressed why we weren't seeing results —we needed more boldness and more prayer. He really got specific, like if people ask you where you're going, you don't say 'to a meeting,' or 'to I-V,' but 'to Inter-Varsity Christian Fellowship.' Let them know who you are."

Tied in here is a chapter goal "to promote the believers' expectancy of the Lord's harvest." There must be faith to believe God is bringing people to himself now and where they live A year ago the chapter held a campus mission—one concentrated week of intense outreach evangelism. Thousands of hours of preparation went into the mission and perhaps fifteen hundred people heard the gospel in some fairly clear way, with twelve to fourteen making a decision for Christ. All efforts like this can **149** become a temptation to walk away from the job after it is over. "That's our evangelism for now." It is to counter that tendency that special efforts have been made to stress the harvest this year.

Training by example, actually going with a person to share the gospel, gives some direction to the boldness. "We don't force-feed people," a chapter officer told me. "Evangelism is so involved with confrontation that there must be a desire on the person's part to get the training he needs and to pay the price in learning it." This takes some initiative from the more mature Christians on campus to encounter the newer ones and tutor them. An annual evangelism training series will cover the material, but the real training comes in the follow-up during the weeks after, when genuine witnessing experiences put the knowledge to work.

The Miami chapter uses all the standard witness aids. The famed "bridge illustration," a diagram of the plan of salvation that shows Christ as the bridge to God, has been taught to many students as a useful way of explaining the gospel. Dorm evangelistic meetings are used but, as always, they depend on an existing Christian witness to credibly go over and to get a crowd out. Booktables are set up every three weeks or so in the union. Inter-Varsity camps and conferences, books and HIS magazines —all make a contribution. Christian faculty are deeply involved, offering their time and gifts for use within the chapter. But no slick tricks are here. Nothing but prayer, obedience, hard work and older Christians training younger ones.

"I think we often settle for too little in our chapters," Barney Ford said. "We expect sustained chapters of thirty to sixty people when we could touch many more. We're praying here for forty kids to get to Student Leadership Training camps next summer. These are month-long training camps that emphasize all the basics of the Christian life; I don't think any campus in the country has seen so many students getting that kind of preparation to make the chapter go.

"But numbers are often irrelevant and intimidating. I bring them in here simply to stimulate some vision in other chapters for what they might be in two or three years if they'll dig in and abandon get-big-quick schemes. The Miami chapter had about thirty active people four years ago; now they are in motion with one hundred fifty to two hundred."

"I just stood back and watched God do it," one girl mentioned to me, describing the growth of the chapter. But in reality she was right in the middle of God's doing it—one of the most active influences to Christ on the campus. Such is the confession of faith: Those God uses most always credit him for the results.

C. Stephen Board is executive editor of Eternity *magazine. He was formerly on Inter-Varsity staff in Chicago and editor of* HIS *magazine.*

TOOLS
FOR
EVANGELISM

The following books are grouped into three categories. The first consists of *books* which discuss various issues in depth which you or a non-Christian friend may be interested in. The second lists *booklets* which give a capsule summary of many of these issues. The third category is for Christians. It lists books which deal with evangelistic strategy or give further help toward an effective witness. In each of the three categories, the more general and basic books are listed first, the more specific and complex books last.

books to be read and given to non-christian friends

John R. W. Stott. *Basic Christianity.* 2nd ed. Downers Grove, Illinois: InterVarsity Press, 1971. A classic summary of the content of Christianity, covering who Christ is, what he has done, people's need in the face of sin and how they can respond to God. A great refresher for the believer and a clear presentation for the seeker.

C. S. Lewis. *Mere Christianity*. New York: Macmillan, 1952. With clear writing and compelling logic, Lewis brings together insights into the essentials of Christianity. A good general book for the thinking person.

Francis Schaeffer. *Escape from Reason* and *The God Who Is There*. Downers Grove, Illinois: InterVarsity Press, 1968. Both books offer a critique of the philosophical basis of 20th-century culture. The first emphasizes the effect of the dualism introduced by Aquinas on modern forms of mysticism, while the second analyzes art, philosophy, music and literature, showing how God has died in our world and how man has followed him into the grave. For the philosophically minded.

Paul E. Little. *Know Why You Believe*. Downers Grove, Illinois: InterVarsity Press, 1968. This book gives readable answers to many of the basic questions people ask about God, Christ, his resurrection, the reliability of the Bible, miracles, science, the problem of evil and other religious and Christian experiences.

Michael Green. *Runaway World*. Downers Grove, Illinois: InterVarsity Press, 1968. An answer to the charge that Christianity is just another form of escapism with strong critiques of the major arguments against it. Excellent for skeptical seekers.

R. T. France. *I Came to Set the World on Fire*. Downers Grove, Illinois: InterVarsity Press, 1975. If you or a friend wants to focus attention on the life, character and message of Jesus of Nazareth, here is an excellent and readable study.

Frank Morison. *Who Moved the Stone?* Downers Grove, Illinois: InterVarsity Press, 1956. An exciting look at the events surrounding the resurrection. Here are the results of an investigation of the resurrection by a lawyer who expected negative conclusions but was brought to faith by the facts themselves.

F. F. Bruce. *The New Testament Documents: Are They Reliable?* 5th ed. Downers Grove, Illinois: InterVarsity Press, 1960. For those with questions about the reliability and accuracy of the New Testament, the author carefully sifts the historical evidence for their reliability.

J. B. Phillips. *The Ring of Truth.* New York: Macmillan, 1967. If you or a friend questions the validity of Christianity and the Scriptures, read this author's story of renewed confidence in both, as he translated the New Testament.

Hugh Silvester. *Arguing with God.* Downers Grove, Illinois: InterVarsity Press, 1971. A carefully reasoned analysis of the problem of evil in the world for Christians who assume that God is all good.

C. S. Lewis. *Out of the Silent Planet* trilogy and the *Chronicles of Narnia.* New York: Macmillan. Fiction can be one of the most delightful and compelling avenues to truth. Through this science-fiction trilogy and set of children's books, Lewis directs the reader to the Source of all truth.

James W. Sire. *The Universe Next Door.* Downers Grove, Illinois: InterVarsity Press, 1976. Clear definitions of theism, deism, naturalism, nihilism, existentialism, Eastern mysticism and the new consciousness, with an explanation of why Christian theism is still the best option for modern man.

Os Guinness. *The Dust of Death.* Downers Grove, Illinois: InterVarsity Press, 1973. A solid critique of cultural developments in the last thirty years, covering humanism, futurology, political radicalism, Eastern mysticism, drugs and the occult, with a proposal for a way out of personal despair and cultural death.

C. Stephen Evans. *Despair—A Moment or a Way of Life?* Downers Grove, Illinois: InterVarsity Press, 1971. If you or a friend has been troubled by existential literature, here's the journey of a modern man through despair to a kind of hope not founded on escape but on a reality more real than anything this side of despair.

booklets to be read and given to non-christian friends

(All of the following are available from InterVarsity Press, Downers Grove, Illinois 60515.)

John W. Alexander. *What Is Christianity?* A clear presentation of the essence of Christianity for someone wanting a capsule summary.

Kenneth Taylor. *Is Christianity Credible?* Answers to

arguments often used by skeptics, atheists and agnostics trying to "disprove" Christianity.

John R.W. Stott. *Becoming a Christian*. A brief but complete discussion of man's fundamental problem and the Christian answer to it, outlining the meaning of Christianity and suggesting specific steps a person can take to respond to God's truth.

Robert Munger. *My Heart–Christ's Home*. Many have come to Christ or been strengthened in their faith in him through this comparison of Christ's place in an individual's life to an owner's possession of his home. The need for a Christian to be wholeheartedly devoted to the One who owns him is made clear.

Howard Guinness. *The Man They Crucified*. A concise look at Jesus, and the meaning and necessity of his death for humanity.

Masumi Toyotome. *Three Kinds of Love*. Through a look at the different kinds of love humans have for each other, the author emphasizes the great love God has expressed for people in the selfless love of his Son.

The Western Book of the Dead. A witty, incisive, twelve-chaptered entire history of man. Great as an evangelistic conversation starter.

J. N. D. Anderson. *The Evidence for the Resurrection*. A discussion of the historical validity of the events involved in Jesus' resurrection.

V. Mary Stewart. *Sexual Freedom*. A young professor of psychology recounts the sexual revolution which took place in her own life after she became a Christian and testifies to the relevance of the Christian sex ethic for today. Shows the relevance of Christianity for those who think it is only in your head and not in the way you live as well.

Brian Maiden. *One Way to God?* An often-asked question is whether Jesus Christ is really the only way to God. Here is an answer especially in the light of alternative positions such as Buddhism, Hinduism and Islam.

Edwin Yamauchi. *Jesus, Zoroaster, Buddha, Socrates, Muhammad*. This specialist in near-Eastern religion presents a parallel discussion of five major religious leaders —including each one's birth, teachings and death—all of which highlights the uniqueness of Christ.

David Haddon. *Transcendental Meditation.* For Christians or non-Christians who think TM is simply a physical relaxation technique, this explanation shows how TM finds its roots in Hinduism and actually contradicts the Christian message. A Christian response closes the booklet.

J. Isamu Yamamoto. *The Moon Doctrine.* If you or a friend has questions about Sun Myung Moon and his Unification Church, this booklet exposes the true religious foundations of this cult.

more reading on evangelism

Paul E. Little. *How to Give Away Your Faith.* Downers Grove, Illinois: InterVarsity Press, 1966. You know the message and you're motivated, but you need help on just *how* to start a conversation, answer questions and call to commitment. Paul Little serves up some suggestions. A group guide with 9-18 studies is available separately.

Robert Coleman. *Master Plan of Evangelism.* Old Tappan, New Jersey: Revell, 1963. Frustrated by the immensity of the evangelistic task? The author explains Jesus' own plan for evangelizing and discipling.

J. I. Packer, *Evangelism and the Sovereignty of God.* Downers Grove, Illinois: InterVarsity Press, 1961. Some people think that the complete sovereignty of God eliminates our responsibility to spread the Good News. J. I. Packer says No and explains why clearly and biblically.

Kenneth F. W. Prior. *The Gospel in a Pagan Society.* Downers Grove, Illinois: InterVarsity Press, 1975. How can the gospel speak to contemporary trends and philosophies? This book uses Paul's Mars Hill sermon (Acts 17) to show how.

William E. York. *One to One.* Downers Grove, Illinois: InterVarsity Press, 1972. Using the Bible itself is one of the best ways to talk to someone who wants to know more about Jesus. These six brief studies cover the essentials of the gospel and open the door for commitment.

Ada Lum. *How to Begin an Evangelistic Bible Study.* Downers Grove, Illinois: InterVarsity Press, 1971. While *One to One* is an actual Bible study to be used with non-Christians, this book by Ada Lum gives general principles Christians can use for initiating and leading evangelistic

Bible studies with their friends.

John R.W. Stott. *The Authority of the Bible*. Downers Grove, Illinois: InterVarsity Press, 1974. "Why do you believe the Bible?" you're asked. You needn't run from the question; this booklet outlines the basis of trust in Scripture.

Richard Peace. *Witness*. Grand Rapids, Michigan: Zondervan, 1971. Here is a week-by-week guide for a small group wanting to learn about evangelism in theory and practice. A leader's study guide is available separately.

Colin Chapman. *Christianity on Trial*. Wheaton, Illinois: Tyndale, 1975. This source book on apologetics puts at your disposal the essential thoughts of scholars and philosophers (Christian and non-Christian) on Christianity. Worth every dime.

Bernard Ramm. *Protestant Christian Evidences*. Chicago: Moody Press, 1954. Ready for a comprehensive presentation on Christian apologetics? The author argues that prophecy, miracles, Jesus' character and resurrection, and Christian experience verify Christian truth.

FELLOWSHIP BIBLE CHURCH
16391 CHILLICOTHE ROAD
CHAGRIN FALLS, OH 44023-4323